PAINTING LANDSCAPES with
atmosphere
RAY BALKWILL

an artist's essential guide

D&C
David and Charles

A DAVID & CHARLES BOOK
Copyright © David & Charles Limited 2006

David & Charles is an F+W Publications Inc. company
4700 East Galbraith Road
Cincinnati, OH 45236

First published in the UK in 2006

Text and illustrations copyright © Ray Balkwill 2006

A catalogue record for this book is available from the
British Library.

ISBN-13: 978-0-7153-2292-5 hardback
ISBN-10: 0-7153-2292-3 hardback

ISBN-13: 978-0-7153-2301-4 paperback (USA only)
ISBN-10: 0-7153-2301-6 paperback (USA only)

Printed in China by SNP Leefung
for David & Charles
Brunel House   Newton Abbot   Devon

Commissioning Editor Freya Dangerfield
Project Editor Ian Kearey
Assistant Editor Louise Clark
Art Editor Sarah Underhill
Production Controller Kelly Smith
Photography by Nigel Cheffers-Heard

Visit our website at www.davidandcharles.co.uk

David & Charles books are available from all good
bookshops; alternatively you can contact our Orderline
on 0870 9908222 or write to us at FREEPOST EX2
110, D&C Direct, Newton Abbot, TQ12 4ZZ (no stamp
required UK only); US customers call 800-289-0963
and Canadian customers call 800-840-5220.

Contents

Introduction

'The only real voyage of discovery consists not in seeking new landscapes, but in having new eyes.'
MARCEL PROUST

Even before reading this, I expect you have already flicked through the pages to look at the paintings – after all, this is something we all do when we first pick up a new book.

Painting is a result of experiences, and this book is about a personal response to the landscape, a celebration of the wonders of nature in paint. It is a journey that will take us to some of my favourite painting locations, both in the UK and abroad, from the rugged coastline and picturesque fishing harbours of Cornwall to the wild mountains and tumbling waterfalls of Wales, and from the sheltered estuaries of Brittany to the sunlit vineyards of Italy. This book, however, is much more than my travels through the landscape to record what I see in paint. It is also about an inner journey, one that involves developing a connection and understanding with the landscape before painting it.

The formative years

Like countless artists before me, landscapes have always attracted, absorbed and hypnotized me for as long as I can remember. My passion for nature as well as art goes back to my childhood, which was spent in a small market town on the very edge of the rugged moorland of Dartmoor. The boulder-strewn rivers that tumbled off the moor into the verdant valleys and rich Devon farmland were my playground, and I think the freedom, mystery and unpredictability have stayed with me ever since.

Pounding Surf
Watercolour and pastel
36 x 53cm (14 x 21in)
I love the sea in all its moods, particularly scenes like this with thundering waves crashing onto rugged rocks. Watercolour combined with pastel is the perfect medium for capturing this.

Interpreting the landscape

Painting is, of course, open to individual interpretation, and every artist has his or her own views; therefore it is my own personal viewpoint that I put across, based on observation and first-hand experience rather than art training. I class myself very much as a self-taught painter with a natural efficiency for art – I believe that there are only a few basic rules in painting and that the real perception of art comes not from the artist, but from the viewer. When I first started painting watercolours, realism was the most important consideration in my work. However, as time went on, I became less enamoured with this and found myself wanting to paint with more expression and feeling for the subject.

My artistic journey has led me to work in most media, and I feel my work has developed over the years through experiment and exploration. Seeking out new subjects

Painting in Newquay harbour

Moorland Falls
Watercolour and pastel
36 x 53cm (14 x 21in)
The brooding atmosphere of storm clouds enveloping mountains is irresistible.

and experiencing the vastly different qualities of light and landscape to be found further afield, has always played an important part in this development. However, I still firmly believe that an artist can paint his own land better than anywhere else – after all, artists who have chosen to paint the land because they love it are bound to paint the best landscapes, and having lived beside both sea and estuary for the past 25 years, it is hardly surprising that these subjects hold a special appeal for me.

Past masters

One can learn a great deal by examining the work of past and contemporary master painters and analysing each artist's individual approach to the subject. Painters throughout the centuries have attempted to unravel the wonders of the landscape around them.

The tradition of landscape painting is built on detail, figuration and romance, and early painters such as Claude Lorrain (1600–82) often told stories around their landscapes. Lorrain was a romantic painter, much of whose subject matter centred around classical mythology – many of his paintings were narratives for which the landscape, often completely imaginary, was merely a setting.

This was all to change when J.M.W. Turner (1775–1851) came on the scene. Turner admired, and early on was

Sunlit Water, Topsham
Watercolour
36 x 25cm (14 x 10in)
The fluidity and transparency of watercolour make it the ideal medium for painting 'soft' atmospheric river scenes such as this.

influenced by Lorrain's paintings; however, he developed his own visions and soon became the most innovative painter of his time. Turner was a great advocate of painting *en plein air* and would go to great lengths to capture the light and atmosphere of a particular scene.

It was the paintings of John Constable (1776–1837) that were to epitomize the atmosphere of the English landscape in paint. His paintings were a response to and love, born out of a lifelong acquaintance and a profound sense of belonging, of his native landscape.

The Impressionists took landscape painting to another dimension. For Claude Monet (1840–1926), this meant working directly from nature, evoking its light and atmosphere through colour and touch. His paintings encompassed movement, spontaneity and sensuality.

The experience and intimacy of landscape is a central theme to many more recent artists whose work I also admire: masters of their art, such as Edward Seago and Rowland Hilder, as well as Trevor Chamberlain, Kurt Jackson and John Virtue, who continue in the tradition of recreating both what they see and what they feel.

Using this book

Painting Landscapes with Atmosphere is designed to show you how I tackle a subject, from the initial inspiration, through exploring with the sketchbook, to the finished picture. Each chapter deals with a different aspect of the landscape, from skies to estuaries and from mountains to seascapes. The book also encompasses a wide range of media, including watercolour, pastels, oils and mixed media. This is not only because I feel that some subjects lend themselves to one particular medium over another, but it may also encourage you to experiment and develop your own ability further.

Within each chapter there are tips on sketching materials and choosing a painting medium, as well as some expert advice on each subject. The 'Feature Pages'

Rain-washed Sky over Courtlands
Oils
25 x 36cm (10 x 14in)
Such exciting lighting conditions can come about with little warning, so always carry a sketchbook to record these fleeting moments.

highlight particular areas of painting, such as tone, drawing boats, and composition, and give answers to many common questions. In each 'Diary Showcase' you can accompany me on some painting trips and share my experiences of working on location. With the emphasis on practical instruction, the detailed step-by-step demonstrations give a deeper insight into the thinking and working processes of how a professional artist goes about creating a painting. At the end of each chapter follows a 'Gallery' of paintings, which I hope will provide an invaluable source of ideas to inspire you further in your own painting.

Sunset on the Exe
Watercolour and pastel
43 x 46cm (17 x 18in)
Here I employed a simple palette of complementary colours and combined watercolour and pastel to produce a painting of bold contrasts and effects.

Four Essentials for Capturing Atmosphere

Let us begin by looking briefly at what I believe to be the four main ingredients for painting landscapes with atmosphere. These are: working on location, emotion, tone and colour, in that order.

Painting on location

Working *en plein air* is not always easy, but it is the one main essential; it is also by far the most satisfying. To paint any landscape well means getting to know it before painting it. This involves not only looking at the landscape, but also walking through it. We must feel it, listen to it and smell it – in fact, we must absorb our whole self in it, whether it is a cold winter day in the mountains or a hot summer day on the coast. We must enter the landscape like explorers searching out the essence of the scene and all that it has to offer – and more than once! Painting on location is my first love, and each time I set up my easel on location, I feel very privileged indeed to be there doing what I do.

When painting on site I try to complete a painting in one sitting, which can be anything between two and four hours – this is the maximum time limit before the light changes dramatically. Paintings that are interrupted by the weather and are unfinished rarely get completed in the studio – I find it difficult to return to these once I am away from the scene, so they are stored in a drawer and regarded as reference sketches. I also find working against the light (*contre-jour*) exciting, as it can make far more dramatic paintings, as well as being easier to paint with the support shaded from a bright sun.

Roddino, Piemonte, Italy
Watercolour and pastel
36 x 53cm (14 x 21in)
The intense light, strong contrast of bright colours, and variety of textures found in the landscape made watercolour combined with pastel the obvious choice of medium.

Interpreting with your heart

Technique without feeling offers little more than a temporary attraction, so painting also involves an inward journey. It means looking deeper emotionally – an interaction between spirit, soul and the subject. A painting must be skilful, but it also needs the vital ingredient of passion if it is to touch the viewer's imagination and sensitivity. The emotion then must come out through the paint and how it is applied. Every landscape has its own uniqueness, so to understand it fully means getting under the skin of a place: it means finding out more about its inhabitants, its history and how it has evolved.

Looking deeper emotionally is what artists call a 'sense of place', and to me this is as important as the painting process itself. It is this personal as well as physical relationship with the land that is so important. D.H. Lawrence once said that 'The spirit of place is a great reality'. Capturing that 'spirit' and intimacy with the landscape is something I strive for in my paintings.

The importance of tone

Achieving mood and depth through tonal value is a vitally important ingredient, and once you begin to recognize the various tonal values in a subject, your paintings will take a major step forwards.

I cannot stress enough the great importance of sketching in mono-chrome, particularly in a medium such as charcoal. It will not only help develop your powers of observation, but also sharpen your awareness of seeing tone in colour. Tonal value is your most important tool for holding a painting to-gether, so learn to master it effectively and build your confidence.

Colour supports the mood

When I look at a scene, the first question I ask myself is 'What is its mood, and which medium would best portray this?' With colour, I look for the most dominant, often referred to as the 'mother colour'. I also ask myself what is the overall temperature – is it warm or cool? Using this principle will connect the shapes throughout the painting and help to unify it.

There are many excellent books available on colour, so the subject is not explicitly covered in this book. However, my thoughts and observations are given on these matters where relevant.

Understanding the basic principles of colour mixing is essential, but it is also possible to get caught up in theory at the cost of personal expression. My own colour sense relies as much on intuition as anything else, and my main concern is to paint what colours I see as well as feel are right for the subject.

I believe that often too much thinking about colour mixing can inhibit the way the painting is expressed. Cezanne once said, 'When I start thinking, everything is lost.' He also said, 'Painting from nature is not copying the object; it is realizing one's sensations.' If you like a colour combination, forget the colour theory – just paint it!

Throughout this book you will see my paintings done in completely contrasting conditions throughout the world, as well as in a range of different media. Learning how to observe and then translate these in paint is what this book is about.

I have found that some mediums work better than others for creating atmosphere of course, but all can be adapted with various techniques. For example, for creating a soft and gentle

Morning Mist
Watercolour
13 x 18cm (5 x 7in)
Watercolour lends itself perfectly to the pearly atmosphere of a misty river scene. Its tints and overlaying washes create a mood that no other medium can achieve.

mood, watercolour is an ideal medium, as illustrated above in *Morning Mist*: the soft edges and closely related tonal values recreate the rising mist on the river perfectly. In contrast, the hot, bright conditions of *Below Cissone, Piemonte*, opposite, done in mixed media (watercolour and pastel), resulted in a painting of warm colours with sharp, high contrasts of vastly different tonal value. Other paintings fall between these two extremes and sit in the medium-contrast range.

Much of this book is concerned with my own instinctive response to a landscape, the way the scene made me feel, and the media and techniques that I employed to capture it. However, there are no rules or formulas to follow; after all, the initial experience, emotion and weather are never the same. Each different landscape presents its own problems, and no matter how many times I go back to a location, there are always going to be fresh challenges to face – which is why the endless quest is so exhilarating!

CHAPTER ONE

Materials

Painting with pastels in the studio.

Equipment for painting on location in watercolour and pastel, including my Herring Versatile easel, carrying folder and stool.

Each medium has its own characteristics and visual qualities, and you may have already explored and developed your own preferences. Whether it's the delicacy of watercolour, the immediacy of pastels or the richness of oils, exploring the qualities each medium has to offer is a very rewarding experience.

I am often asked what is my favourite medium, and my answer is 'the one that I am using at the time' as a scene may lend itself to one particular medium. It's not that one medium is more attractive or better than another, but it's about my own personal response to the subject. I also find it stimulating to frequently change media, as this helps to keep my paintings fresher and more alive.

Experimenting in mixed media is another way of extending your range of artistic expression: for example, I find the combination of watercolour and soft pastel particularly exciting. It is the great diversity of effects that intrigues me, and the combinations are endless.

Equipment

Planning what to take is essential, and as I am a strong advocate of painting *en plein air*, keeping my equipment simple and portable is very important. The following is by no means a comprehensive guide, but my own choice of materials and working methods. As with everything associated with the painting process, try to keep your materials and equipment as simple as possible.

For watercolour and pastel work I use a Herring Versatile easel, which is extremely light and has the advantage of being able to be folded flat. I have a shoulder bag for carrying my materials, which I hang on the easel with a hook to help stabilize the easel in blustery weather conditions. I take a zip-carrying folder, which carries my stool, drawing board and sketchbook; the folder also makes a useful table for materials when placed on the stool when painting on location. For oils I use a folding box easel that carries paints and brushes.

I use a radial studio easel for painting in the studio; occasionally when working in watercolour I sit at a table and tilt a desk easel at 45 degrees. For quick drying I use a hairdryer, and if I am not working with natural light I find a daylight-simulation easel lamp useful.

Drawing media

Given the vast range of drawing media – both wet and dry – that is available, it is worth taking the time to experiment with as many different types as possible, to find what suits your style of working best.

Grades 2B and 4B graphite pencils are ideal for most drawing work, and watersoluble graphite and coloured pencils can produce interesting effects, such as when making quick tonal sketches.

I enjoy combining drawing media together too, in order to obtain certain effects, in particular ballpoint pen, felt-tip pen and pencil. But my favourite sketching medium has to be willow charcoal, available in sticks of varying thickness, as well as in pencil form; this is a wonderfully expressive medium that is invaluable for working quickly and capturing mood and atmosphere. You can also combine charcoal with black and white conté pencils or crayons, and even felt-tip pens.

Felt- or fibre-tip pens are either permanent or watersoluble, and there is a wide range of tips. However, many of these pens may not be lightfast, so experiment with them before you settle on what you want to use.

For charcoal sketches I use A3 cartridge pads of 135gsm (60lb), and I use smaller hardback sketchbooks in a landscape format of approximately 23 x 30cm (9 x 11in) for pencil and watercolour sketches. My other drawing equipment includes hard and soft putty erasers, a sharp craft knife and a spray can of fixative.

Watercolour

Watercolour's wonderful properties of, translucency, expressiveness and unpredictability make it a very exciting medium for artists to use.

As with most art materials today, a great choice of watercolour papers is available, so you should experiment until you find your favourites; most types are available in pochette, or small swatch, form, which makes inexpensive comparisons easy to make. I move between 300gsm (140lb) Whatman, Saunders Waterford, Arches, Bockingford and Fabriano paper, either Not (Cold Pressed) or Rough, stretched on to a drawing board with gummed tape. My drawing boards are 56 x 66cm (22 x 30in) and 41 x 58cm (16 x 23in), which are ideal for a quarter- and a half-imperial sheet of paper respectively.

Watercolour brushes range from the very expensive Kolinsky sable, through other sables, blends of sable and synthetic, and squirrel hair, to inexpensive pure synthetics. I typically use a 2.5cm (1in) hake, a No. 12 round synthetic-sable mix, a No. 14 filbert and a No. 1 rigger, and supplement this selection when necessary.

I use tubes of artists'-quality paint, squeezed out into a paintbox or on to a large plastic palette and several porcelain plates. My standard palette is cadmium red, permanent rose, light red, burnt umber, burnt sienna, raw sienna, ultramarine blue, cerulean blue, cobalt blue, phthalo blue (red shade), cadmium yellow, lemon yellow, Naples yellow and cadmium orange, and I also use viridian, indigo and cobalt blue to achieve certain mixes and effects.

I also make use of a plastic ruler, kitchen roll, masking fluid, a sponge and a roll of masking tape, depending on the painting. For location painting, I take a small plastic bottle of water and a collapsible lantern water pot with me.

Gouache

Gouache is water-based, but it is more opaque than watercolour – hence its other name of body colour – drying to a chalky matt finish. In addition to being used as a medium in its own right, gouache can be combined with watercolour to give highlights, solidity and contrast. Its opacity means that you do not have to rely on the whiteness of the paper to provide highlights, as with watercolour; it can also be thinned with water to a fluid consistency. It can be applied to a wide variety of supports, but is perhaps more effective when applied on a coloured pastel paper or mountboard.

My own choice is Canson Mi-Teintes pastel paper, which I stretch onto a board with gummed brown paper tape.

Gouache tends to harden more quickly in tubes than watercolour; a useful tip is to squeeze the colour up into the tube after use to dispel any air. If the paints are not to be used for long periods, it is also helpful to store the tubes by standing them upright on their caps.

Watercolour brushes are the best to use with gouache, and my range of colours includes Naples yellow, warm grey, cool grey, flesh tint and brown pink and permanent white, all of which can be combined well with watercolours.

Oils

Oils are immediately attractive, due to their smooth, rich, buttery consistency. To save time, you can also combine oils and acrylics, using the quicker drying time of the acrylics to make an underpainting, over which oils can then be applied.

All sorts of supports are available for oils, from prestretched canvas to tear-off disposable pads of oil paper. For many of the paintings in this book, as well as the project in oils, I used MDF (medium-density fibreboard) primed with two coats of gesso and then a final coat mixed with an equal amount of texture paste; for the most part, my board sizes are 35 x 25cm (14 x 10in) and 35 x 35cm (14 x 14in).

When it comes to brushes for oils, my personal preference is for softer brushes, such as Daler-Rowney Dalon rounds and flats, but the most important thing is to have a good choice of shapes, and you should experiment with both these softer brushes and traditional harder hoghair ones until you find what works for you.

I mix my colours on a traditional mahogany palette, with the warm colours on one side and the cool on the other; laying out your colours in the same order each time you paint can save valuable time. I use both artists' – and students' – quality paints, with a standard palette of raw sienna, burnt sienna, ultramarine blue, cerulean blue, rose madder, cadmium red, Naples yellow, cadmium yellow, viridian and titanium white; I will also use cadmium lemon yellow, cobalt violet, cadmium orange, light red and burnt umber when required.

Within easy reach I also have turpentine, a palette knife and plenty of clean rags, and I use a bar of soap for cleaning brushes.

Pastels

Soft pastels bridge the gap between drawing and painting, but tend to be regarded commonly as a painting medium. However they are viewed, their great advantage is that they are light and portable, and, being dry, they provide an immediate effect, without the problems found in paints, primarily drying speed and colour mixing on the palette.

Pastels manufacturers make a wide range of tints and shades, and there is no problem about mixing and matching between brands: my own pastel box includes pastels from pretty well all the well-known brands. (When working on location, however, I use fewer colours – as many as can be carried in a few small boxes.)

Faced with such a huge number of shades, it can be difficult to know where to start building up a palette – a light, medium and dark pastel of each colour gives good results and won't break the bank. I always remove the labels from my pastels, but only after making a colour chart with reference numbers alongside the colours; this is particularly handy when it comes to renewing my pastels.

I use Not-surfaced watercolour paper and tinted pastel papers for the most part, but there is a wide variety of alternatives available, ranging from sugar paper to pastel papers, boards and glasspaper. When trying out supports for pastels, remember that the tooth, or texture, is as important a consideration as the colour and tonal value.

The disadvantage of pastels is that they remain chalky and dusty, and they can be smudged easily until they have been set with fixative, usually from a spray can. I happen not to fix my pastels, while other artists spray while their painting is in progress, leaving the top layer of pastel unsprayed – but there are no rules of what to do or not to do. To get over the problem of smudging while working on location, I tape a piece of newspaper over the painting to prevent movement.

Hard pastels, pastel pencils and conté crayons are all useful for adding detail and working in small areas of a painting. In addition, I use a container of ground rice in which to clean the pastels, tissues for blending, and a hoghair brush for correcting mistakes.

CHAPTER TWO

Sources of Inspiration

'Painting is one per cent inspiration and ninety-nine per cent perspiration.'
J.M.W. TURNER

For me, there is nothing more exhilarating and inspirational than sketching or painting *en plein air*, trying to capture the special atmosphere of a scene. 'Get inspired, get organized and then get going' I tell students on courses when we arrive at a painting spot. However, inspiration comes not only from looking around, but also from inside one's self as well.

When I paint it is on two levels: I am painting not only what I see, but also what I feel. Whatever it may be, it is this first response to the scene and the contact between you and the subject that is so important in what is to follow.

Being excited and enthusiastic about a subject is a prerequisite for creating a successful painting. Sometimes the inspiration finds you, then at other times you have to work harder and search to find it. This may be on a grand scale, such as a dramatic sky, and at other times it may be much simpler – a reflection in a tide pool, for instance.

Painting has to encompass all the senses; it is also about emotion, and this is something you have to experience at first hand. This joy of the subject helps implant the 'spirit' of what you feel and see.

**The Harbour,
Lympstone**
Pen and charcoal
30 x 38cm (12 x 15in)
*This atmospheric sketch
not only captures the
atmosphere of a scene,
but also helps resolve
a number of priorities,
such as composition,
centre of interest and
tonal values.*

Drawing and understanding

Drawing is first and foremost about awareness – letting your hand draw what you see, what you think and what you feel. This is a necessary foundation skill for painting – after all, painting is no more than simply drawing with a brush – and to achieve the best results one must sketch at every opportunity.

Like the painting process itself, an artist's sketchbook can take on many forms and is all about individual interpretation. The marks you make are the visual language you use to tell the story to the viewer. A sketch not only sets down the memory of an experience, but can also help to understand the subject better and improve your drawing and observational skills.

Sketchbooks are vital for gathering information, which then allows you to reconnect with the subject in the studio. A sketchbook can also take the form of a scrapbook, in which photographs, found materials and experiments are collated to help provide ideas. But most importantly, a sketchbook gives you the opportunity to practise and improve your observational and drawing skills.

Before starting, it is important to consider a number of points, for instance, which medium might be best suited for the particular subject, how much time is available, and what you wish to achieve: gathering information or capturing atmosphere. My own type of sketching can be broken down into two basic types, which are described overleaf.

Mullion Cove
Pen and watercolour
13 x 15cm (5 x 6in)
*I often use a small hardback
sketchbook for pen or pencil
combined with watercolour
to gather information.*

Information sketches

These are about gathering information from the scene as *aides-memoire*. They tend to be carefully observed monochrome drawings done in graphite pencil, often accompanied by notes. If I require colour reference, I sometimes sketch in felt-tip pen, ballpoint or pencil, and add watercolour washes in a hardback sketchbook. However, most of my colour references are what I call 'location studies' – sketches that usually take about an hour, done in watercolour and gouache on prestretched sheets of mid-tone tinted pastel paper.

Atmosphere sketches

Quick monochrome impressions play a vital role in exploring tonal relationships and particular moods. For these sketches I use a broader medium, such as sticks of willow charcoal combined with felt-tip pens, in an A3 cartridge sketchbook. They are done quite quickly, taking no longer than 30 minutes at the most, and sometimes are accompanied by written notes to remind me of the colours in the scene.

Watersoluble pencils and pens are useful for quick tonal studies, either on their own or combined with charcoal, and pastels can help to capture skies and fleeting moments of light. Whatever you use, try to obtain contrast and sparkle in your drawing.

Studio painting

Because of the techniques they use, many artists prefer to paint in the studio in a more considered approach from their sketches, than to work on location. I find that when I am studio-based, my paintings tend to tighten up and become more detailed. To overcome this problem I not only set myself a time limit – a similar time scale to when I am painting outside

Mousehole Harbour
Watercolour
25 x 36cm (10 x 14in)
Using watercolour outdoors can be frustrating – washes dry too quickly on hot days or slowly on damp days. However, these conditions present us with ideal subjects.

Duck Pond, Otterton Mill
Charcoal
28 x 38cm (11 x 15in)
In this sketch the paper was covered with charcoal, which was then blended to achieve a mid tone. Further darks were added, with the highlights being lifted out with a putty eraser.

– but I also paint to music that will help me work quickly. I refer to my sketches as much as possible, as they help to rekindle my passion for the subject.

Photographs are useful, of course, and I don't know any artist who doesn't use them, especially for those fleeting moments. However, the problem with photographs is that they tend to retain too much detail, and the colours can be misleading. This detail is then invariably transferred into your painting, and before you know it, the painting is overworked. The digital camera and computer can be useful tools for the artist too, but do not become over-reliant on photographic references at the cost of your sketchbook. A photograph can never be a substitute for looking hard at the subject and rekindling your feelings in the way a sketch can.

Porthleven Harbour
Watercolour and gouache
36 x 25cm (14 x 10in)
In this location study I chose a contre-jour *(into the light) view to help simplify what would otherwise have been a complex scene.*

Creek at Low Water
Felt-tip pen and charcoal

Shelly Gut is one of my favourite locations on the Exe estuary and one I return to time and again. The creek is steeped in maritime history and still holds on to some of its character, with its traditional boats and colourful boatsheds. I chose this view across the creek to the boatsheds, and in particular liked the position of the three boats in the scene. However, looking over my shoulder I realized that I had to work quickly, as the tide was coming in fast and would totally change the scene – I reckoned I had about 20 minutes before the water would be lapping at my feet!

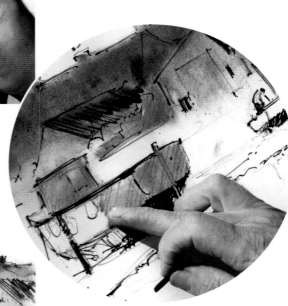

materials

- A3 cartridge pad
- Graphite pencil; black chisel-tip permanent felt-tip marker pen; charcoal sticks; black and white Conté sticks
- Putty eraser

1 I used my viewfinder to help decide on the format, as well as the main elements of the composition (see right). I sketched in the initial outline using a 4B graphite pencil and then worked on this using a broad chisel-tip felt marker pen (see below).

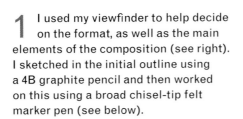

2 Using charcoal on its side I applied the mid tones for the buildings and blended them with my finger (see right). I used this technique for the boat and water, adding further darks using the tip of the charcoal.

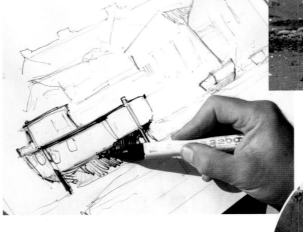

3 To create the lighter areas in the boatsheds and reflections in the water, I lifted off areas of the charcoal with a putty eraser. The figure was added to create life as well as a centre of interest.

4 I put further drawing into the water using charcoal on its side and then blended it with a finger, and used a square black conté stick on its side to create the texture for the beach and on its end to add further details including rope, rigging and television aerials. For the light mast set against the dark roof of the boatshed, I switched to a white conté stick.

Finished Drawing
Creek at Low Water
Felt-tip pen and charcoal
25 x 36cm (10 x 14in)

This demonstration illustrates the importance of working quickly to record a scene that you know will change, particularly if you plan to paint the same scene on location. Sketching with a broad medium such as charcoal is useful for simplifying the scene and arranging the priorities such as composition and tonal values.

The more you work on location, the more you will see. Your powers of observation will be heightened, and your painting satisfaction will increase. No matter how brief a sketch may be, it all helps to build up your practice of co-ordinating hand with eye.

CHAPTER THREE

Atmospheric Skies

Sunlight and Shadow, Dartmoor
Watercolour and pastel
36 x 53cm (14 x 21in)
The changing moods of Dartmoor have always fascinated me; here the scudding clouds cast great swathes of sunlit and shadow areas over the landscape beneath.

'The landscape painter who does not make his skies a very material part of his composition neglects to avail himself of one of his greatest aids.'
JOHN CONSTABLE

Light is the defining factor that can change a landscape from mundane to inspiring in a matter of seconds – and vice versa. It is light that enables us to see colour and form, and these in turn influence the physical and climatic landscapes that make the subject so diverse. The ever-changing light and weather are the factors that ultimately define the character and mood of a place.

Strong observation is the key to understanding these effects, and with practice you can build up a store of information to help you paint them. You don't have to be a meteorologist to paint convincing skies, but it does help to have a basic knowledge of some of the different cloud formations. The character of the sky establishes the mood of a painting and provides an endless source of material.

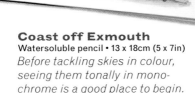

From Dougerie, Isle of Arran
Pencil and watercolour • 13 x 18cm (5 x 7in)
Quick sky studies can play a vital role in exploring and understanding a subject.

Coast off Exmouth
Watersoluble pencil • 13 x 18cm (5 x 7in)
Before tackling skies in colour, seeing them tonally in mono-chrome is a good place to begin.

The sketchbook

The best way to begin your study of skies is by sketching outdoors, devoting a separate sketchbook for this purpose (this was Constable's method). Clouds are constantly on the move, which means working very quickly, so the size you work at, and the drawing media you choose, are important factors.

A sketch can be a quick visual note or a more detailed observation, and can be executed in almost any medium. For small sketches in monochrome, I use watersoluble graphite pencils and pens in a small hardback sketchbook. Tones can be developed simply with a brush and clean water, and I sometimes add touches of colour with ordinary coloured pencils or watercolour pencils.

Pastel pencils are also useful for producing quick studies, and a 23 x 15cm (9 x 6in) sketchbook of Ingres tinted papers is handy. For working larger, I use charcoal in an A3 cartridge pad – the expressive qualities of this medium are ideal for capturing the subtle tonal relationships in skies. One effective technique for quick studies can be achieved by rubbing a middle tone of charcoal on to the paper, then lifting out lighter areas with a putty eraser and adding further dark tones with charcoal.

Choosing a medium

Each medium has its own inherent qualities for portraying the transient effects of nature. Watercolour's soft transparent washes are ideal for suggesting mood and atmosphere, particularly when working wet-in-wet. Gouache is versatile, especially when used on a mid-tone tinted support, such as pastel paper; I use its opacity to create soft, subtle effects, and for painting clouds, I tint tube white with another colour. This also applies to oils, whose rich, impasto quality lends itself particularly to stormy skies or great billowing clouds.

With soft pastel, there is no colour mixing required; when painting skies in pastel, I both blend the colours together with a finger or tissue and use firmer direct marks. Understanding the characteristics of your chosen medium is essential to develop confidence and speed.

Across the Exe
Felt-tip pen, conté crayon and charcoal
28 x 36cm (11 x 14in)
Combining a number of quick media can be useful for capturing dramatic sky effects.

Thoughts about painting skies

Begin by setting the mood and atmosphere of the picture by painting the sky first, and focus on the most interesting part of the sky, rather than putting everything you can see in the picture. It is surprising how many artists treat the sky and landscape as two separate subjects; if you have a busy landscape, keep the sky simple, and vice versa.

Just as there is perspective in a landscape, the same principles apply to clouds, those nearer to us being larger and contrasting more in tone than those further away. You can also see how a blue sky, strong in colour above your head, gets cooler and lighter towards the horizon.

Decide on the colour temperature of the sky – does it have a warm or cool bias? Compare the tonal relationships between the clouds, the sky and the land. You will find that the tones in the sky are always lighter than those in the land – except of course, for a snow-laden landscape.

When painting clouds, always check for the direction of light and look carefully at their structure. When looking *contre-jour*, the clouds will be backlit, with warm colours and bright edges; and when lit from the side, clouds appear three-dimensional, with shadows to one side and below.

Cloud shadows, their reflections in water and subtle plays of light form a vital link within the landscape. In seascapes, too, notice not only how the sky is reflected in the sea and wet sand, but also the way light touches the surface of the sea. When using watercolour, I find it is useful to hold the brush as lightly as possible when painting skies, working with your whole arm rather than just from the wrist.

Skies make an ideal subject for those wishing to loosen up their painting technique. If you are nervous about being faced with a sheet of white paper, try a dry run: before applying paint to the brush, simply sweep the brush over the paper to give a feel of where the paint will go when you do load it.

'Paint a sky a day' was the advice of the great colourist Sir Alfred East, and if you practise doing that you will improve quickly. Remember: be bold, paint with expression and take risks.

Approaching Rain, Benodet
Watercolour • 18 x 25cm (7 x 10in)
Small sketchbook studies are invaluable for capturing the spirit of what you feel, as well as what you see.

Passing Shower, Hay Tor
Watercolour and pastel
41 x 51cm (16 x 20in)
Experiencing different weather conditions and constantly changing light at first hand makes me work with more energy than when painting in the studio.

Connemara, Ireland

Sensation

I had never been to the west coast of Ireland, so when friends offered me their holiday home, I felt it was too good a chance to miss. I knew it would be different, but no one could have prepared me for the beauty of the landscape: big skies, mountains, lochs and an amazing variety of greens. The clarity and quality of the light was inspirational, and every turn in the road presented a new and compelling vista.

A short drive from Outerard, near Galway, is Quiet Man's Bridge. Here I was immediately struck by the view towards the start of the range of mountains that make up the Twelve Bens. The morning was bright but showery, and distant clouds moving across the mountains made a wonderful sight.

The Twelve Bens
This photograph was taken just before I began the painting and clearly shows the scene – the rain came down heavily soon afterwards, a common problem when working outdoors!

Process

Time is a key factor when working outdoors, so I organized my materials, laying out the colours on the palette from light to dark, starting from the right and working around the palette. The main problem was how to portray the mood and grandeur of the place, as well as handling the wide range of greens, including the dominant bright emeralds. I worked on a primed MDF board, prestained with burnt sienna.

My first consideration was deciding which was more important, the sky or the land and water. I decided to play down the sky and concentrate on the colours and light in the landscape, which interested me more; but the first rule I broke was not to place the horizon dead centre! For the greens I decided to use viridian as the base colour, adding red to darken and lemon yellow to lighten the colours.

The Twelve Bens, Connemara
Oils • 33 x 33cm (13 x13in)
This painting is about using both positive and negative shapes to good effect in both sky and landscape. The vertical posts helped to link the landscape together.

Capturing Changing Skies

Painting a sunset or clouds moving across a sky can be a real problem, particularly on a windswept day. Changing your painting as the cloud formations change is not recommended; instead, painting changing skies has to rely on two important factors – keen observation and memory.

Speed, scale and mediums

Whether it is sketching or painting, and whatever medium is chosen, the same urgency is required. For immediacy, soft pastels would be my first choice, as there is no colour mixing required – pastel pencils are also ideal for smaller sketches, such as *Evening Sky* shown below.

Pencil and wash is ideal for working quickly and achieving a 'hard-edged' effect that can be created by working on cartridge paper.

Watercolour remains the most popular medium for painting skies, partly due to being such a portable medium for working on location, but also for its expression and translucency, particularly when working wet-in-wet. However, one of the most effective mediums has to be watercolour and gouache combined. I sometimes use this on a watercolour paper, as in *From Sidari, Corfu*, but more often on a tinted support, such as pastel paper.

Two-minute sketch
Watercolour and gouache on tinted paper
13 x 26cm (5 x 10in)
Using watercolour and gouache on a coloured support can be extremely useful in capturing fleeting skies. For this quick sketch I used a warm mid-tone pastel paper.

From Sidari, Corfu
Watercolour and gouache sketch on watercolour paper
18 x 27cm (7½ x 11in)
Watercolour and gouache proved to be perfect for capturing the soft, hazy light in this landscape.

Evening Sky
Pastel sketch on tinted paper
17 x 19cm (6½ x 7½in)
For speed when painting the changing colours in this sunset, I worked on a small scale using a limited palette of pastels.

Using tinted paper

Some years ago I saw an exhibition of Turner's sketches, which showed his watercolour and body colour work in sketchbooks that he made from folded blue paper. Seeing these confirmed the importance and advantages of working on a tinted support.

For a start, working on a mid-toned paper is less daunting than working on a sheet of white watercolour paper, as it leaves you free to concentrate on the lights and darks; and you will find that with only a few marks applied, the painting grows quickly. It is also less blinding on your eyes when the sun is shining on your paper. Finally, if you leave the colour of the paper untouched in places, this not only saves time but also unifies the picture.

White gouache thinned with water produces a milky wash that suggests the soft colours found in clouds. The semi-transparent colour allows the tint of the paper to show through, adding further subtlety of colour.

Applying opaque gouache very thick and dry, as done here for the highlights on top of the clouds, gives vibrancy and an energetic quality.

Naples yellow watercolour is added to the white gouache for both near and more distant clouds. Perspective also applies to clouds as well as to landscape, those nearer to us being larger and contrasting more in tone than those further away.

The original tone and colour of the paper are left to show through and add an overall unity to the painting. The warm pink paper contrasts with the cooler blues; for a warmer sky, a mid-tone of blue or grey can contrast with warm paints.

Cerulean blue watercolour is added to white gouache to suggest patches of lighter sky. Note also how the sky is stronger in colour immediately above, and gets cooler and lighter towards the horizon.

Billowing Clouds
Watercolour and gouache on tinted pastel paper.
25 x 36cm (10 x 14in)
Skies lend themselves to a combination of an opaque and transparent medium, and gouache and watercolour provide many possibilities. This shows some of the techniques that I use in both quick 'location studies' and more considered paintings.

On the River
Watercolour and gouache

Using watercolour and gouache on a tinted support is a quick way of recording a scene, particularly skies, and is useful as reference material for studio paintings. Working from a felt-tip pen and charcoal sketch of the Exe estuary, I had to rely on memory and experience when it came to the colours and any detail – working this way is stimulating, however, as the results are often surprising. Due to the early evening light, the overall mood was one of warmth and stillness; to echo this I chose a warm mid-tone pastel paper, choosing moonstone Canson Mi-Teintes pastel paper, which contrasted well with the blues and cooler colours of watercolour and gouache.

Reference Sketch
Felt-tip pen and charcoal • 28 x 30cm (11 x 12in)

materials

- Canson Mi-Teintes moonstone pastel paper, stretched

- Watercolours: ultramarine blue, cerulean blue, Naples yellow, permanent rose, cadmium orange, burnt umber, cadmium red; raw sienna

- Gouache: permanent white, warm grey, cool grey

- Brushes: 2.5cm (1in) hake; Nos 6 and 3 round; No. 1 rigger

- 4B pencil

- Plastic ruler

1 For the initial drawing I used a 4B pencil on the smooth side of the prestretched pastel paper. I began by using the 2.5cm (1in) hake brush to wet part of the sky area – not all – and dropped a watercolour mix of ultramarine and cerulean blues on to both the wet and dry areas. While this was wet, I dropped a mix of warm and cool grey gouache and ultramarine, permanent rose and cadmium orange watercolours into the lower part of the sky.

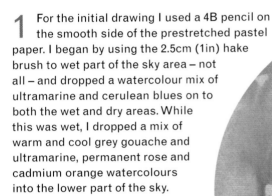

2 I worked down to the horizon line with a mix of all the watercolours used so far, and repeated this in the water at the bottom of the picture, using vertical and horizontal strokes and painting in and around the boats. I then let everything dry.

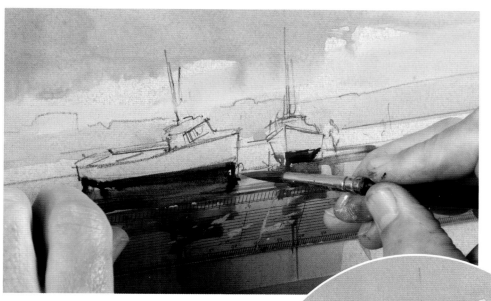

3 To put darks on the boat hulls I used a No. 6 round brush with a mix of ultramarine blue, permanent rose and burnt umber watercolours; for the reflections I added raw sienna to the mix. I used cadmium red with ultramarine for the keel of the right-hand boat, again adding raw sienna to the reflection. To reinforce the shoreline I diluted the brown wash and used a plastic ruler as a mahlstick. I used very light washes of cadmium red and ultramarine blue for the hulls of the boats, and warm grey gouache for the water going up to the shore. For the distant hills I worked wet-into-wet with a cerulean blue and raw sienna mix, and applied bands of ultramarine and permanent rose for the water around the boats, finishing with a drybrush mix of raw sienna watercolour and warm grey gouache.

4 I switched to a No. 3 round brush and pure permanent white gouache for the lightest lights on the boats, which really stand out and help to set the tonal range. With the same brush I used a very dark mix of ultramarine blue and cadmium red for detail on the boats (see right), and then added cerulean blue for the cabin.

Assessment

I was pleased with the overall mood and spontaniety of the picture, so therefore decided that any further work should be confined to the middle distance only. I felt that some further lights were needed on the horizon, in both sky and water. This would not only help link these elements together, but also provide a stronger contrast and recession.

5 I mixed white and warm grey gouache with cerulean blue watercolour and used this fairly dry for the shoreline below the land and on either side of the mudflats. I returned to the dark mix from step 4, using a No. 1 rigger to put in the rigging, masts and sail on the boats.

6 To create recession in the sky, I alternated quick sideways strokes and dabs of two watery mixes – cerulean blue and white gouache, and Naples yellow and white – and repeated this as reflections in the water. I added a further wash of cerulean and permanent rose into the foreground.

7 I continued to add details on and around the boats with the rigger brush and variations on the mixes already used, and added seagulls with white gouache and a No.1 rigger. I added a further wash of cerulean and permanent rose into the foreground. To finish, I put some flicks of 4B pencil on to the rigging.

Finished Painting
On the River
Watercolour and gouache
25 x 36cm (10 x 14in)

Sketching and painting on a toned paper has many advantages. First, it is less daunting than working on white watercolour paper, and second, with just a few marks it can progress more quickly, which is particularly important when painting on location. Another point is that when working in bright sun, there is no glare from white paper to contend with. Above all, it is much easier to assess colours and tones correctly, and you can paint towards light and dark with equal ease.

As here, if you allow the colour of the ground to show through the overpainting in places, as well as applying the colour thinly, this acts as a unifying element. Applied for the lights and darks, the thicker paint makes bold statements and can give the work a strong sense of depth.

Mountain Pass, Connemara
Pastel
25 x 30cm (10 x 12in)
This view is typical of the stunning scenery I encountered in Ireland and was painted with pastels on gold/ochre-coloured Rembrandt board.

(Opposite above)
Last Snow of Winter, Dartmoor
Watercolour and pastel
36 x 53cm (14 x 21in)
A fall of snow can transform the landscape and create a complete reversal of normal tonal relationships, with the snow often lighter than a stormy sky.

(Opposite below)
Cloud over Sail Chalmadale
Oils
25 x 35cm (10 x 14in)
This was painted on a recent trip to the Isle of Arran. I found the solitude and raw beauty of the island absorbing and tried hard to include this in my work.

Evening Fanfare, Exe Estuary
Oils
30 x 36cm (12 x 14in)
Watching the sun go down can be a wonderfully calming experience, but trying to capture it in paint is certainly the opposite. However, don't be timid in front of nature; one must be bold, at the risk of being deceived constantly and making mistakes.

(Opposite above)
Summer Sky, Looe
Watercolour and gouache
25 x 36cm (10 x 14in)
This location study was painted on tinted pastel paper, and retains a transient mood in the scene.

(Opposite below)
Evening Sky, Dartmouth
Watercolour
13 x 18cm (5 x 7in)
This small atmospheric watercolour shows a number of classic watercolour techniques, with the medium lending itself perfectly to the soft evening glow.

CHAPTER FOUR

Rivers and Estuaries

High and Dry
Watercolour
25 x 36cm (10 x 14in)
Achieving the smooth, glassy appearance of calm water requires surprisingly little effort in watercolour.

'Three brushstrokes from nature are worth three day's work in the studio.'

CLAUDE MONET

Whether it is painting on the bank of a wooded river or beside the wide expanse of an estuary, any aspect of water in a picture has a special interest and appeal, and endeavouring to capture it in its many moods is always an exciting and challenging experience.

One place that is particularly special to me and has nourished my creativity for over two decades now is the Exe estuary in south Devon: this is dominated by the tide as the latter sweeps into the estuary to meet the river, and the face of all things constantly changes there. It's a subject I never

tire of, and it provides me with more than enough painting material to last a lifetime.

One artist who was fascinated by water, whether sea, river, or later his own water garden at Giverny, was Monet. It is very reassuring to learn from the hundreds of letters that he wrote, that even he continually struggled to capture what inspired him. In one of his letters he wrote, 'I have started again to paint the impossible: water with waving grass in the background. It is wonderful to look at, but it drives me mad to try and paint it.'

The sketchbook

Quick sketches are an invaluable way of capturing the essentials of both moving and still water.

When scaling up a sketch to develop as a painting, first check that the format is the same and the elements remain in the same relationship to each other. Place the sketch on the paper so that the left-hand side and bottom edge are aligned, then lay a rule diagonally from the bottom left-hand corner to the opposite top right-hand corner. From this, horizontal and vertical lines drawn from the side and bottom of the paper will give you the same format, whatever size you decide on.

Choosing a medium

Watercolour, with its characteristics of translucency and expressiveness, lends itself best to painting water. Calm water requires little effort in watercolour, and letting colours merge together wet-in-wet on dampened paper is perfect for an impression of a misty lake.

Combining watercolour with soft pastels is another favourite medium. When painting in pure pastels I normally work on a tinted support such as pastel paper, particularly if the paper is left to show through in parts. Blending soft pastels is also very effective for showing reflections in water.

River Dart at Spitchwick
Charcoal
28 x 38cm (11 x 15cm)
The richness of charcoal and its capacity to give a wide tonal range is exemplified in this drawing.

River Exe, Topsham
Watercolour and gouache
36 x 25cm (14 x 10in)
In this location study (left) the fragmented reflections attracted me to the scene.

River Avon at Bantham
Pencil and watercolour
18 x 53cm (7 x 21in)
Heavyweight cartridge sketchbooks are ideal for pen, pencil and watercolour.

Painting rivers and estuaries

With watercolour, ripples and reflections can be suggested with a large round brush with a fine point, which can produce calligraphic brushmarks to suggest the water's movement.

For painting movement, a drybrush stroke can suggest highlights or patches of wind-ruffled water. Lifting out colour with a flat brush from a dry wash is also effective. Alternatively, highlights can be reserved on the water's surface with masking fluid, while drybrushing white gouache is yet another method.

The essential characteristic of still water is that it reflects the sky and whatever is close to it in the landscape; and the tone of water is a tone darker than the sky, which increasingly darkens as it gets nearer the viewer.

Reflections always have less intensity of colour and tone than the objects they mirror – reflections of a light boat, for instance, will be reflected darker, and vice versa.

An upright object reflects the same length, but if it leans towards you, it will appear longer; if it leans away, the reflection appears shorter.

Lerryn
Watercolour and gouache
36 x 25cm (14 x 10in)
You need to analyse colours and tones carefully when rendering water. Using tinted pastel paper can help to provide a base for this.

Reflections, River Otter
Watercolour and pastel
45 x 51cm (18 x 20in)
In views painted in a horizontal format, verticals such as trees are important factors.

Sensation

I had been asked to tutor a painting holiday and led an enthusiastic group to the pretty seaside town of Benodet in southern Brittany. We visited many inspiring locations, mainly rivers and estuaries in the area, including the old fishing port of Douarnenez with its floating boat museum.

The first moment of emotional response to a scene is vital, and as soon as I came across the *Providence*, a lovely old Scottish trawler, I knew that this was something I simply had to capture.

What was happening in the water was equally exciting: the surface was disturbed by a strong blustery wind and current, but this was intermittent and when it died down it created calm and reflective passages as well. Between the passing clouds the sun shone through to produce a scene of strong contrasts. In fact the whole scene was very painterly, and I could not wait to get started.

Providence at **Douarnenez, Brittany**
Watercolour and pastel
36 x 53cm (14 x 21in)
To get the best view of this old boat, I started by positioning myself on the end of a narrow walkway, which protruded out into the river. However, the blustery weather made working very difficult, and I retreated to the safety of the bank.

Providence
This photograph shows the scene before I commenced painting.

Process

For this painting I used watercolour and pastel on a prestretched sheet of Bockingford 300gsm (140lb) Not watercolour paper. After sketching out the scene with a waterproof felt-tip pen, I applied masking fluid with an old brush to reserve the movement in the water, and when this was dry I covered the paper with bold washes of watercolour using a 2.5cm (1in) hake and Winsor blue, raw sienna and burnt umber. I built up further darks, particularly in the boat, by adding diluted black waterproof ink to the watercolour mixes.

Having established the overall key and mood of the painting, I applied pastel boldly on its side, making sure to let the watercolour washes show through; this was important where the transparency of the medium was needed, particularly for the water. Little blending was done, as I preferred the more direct marks made with the pastel, which gave more suggestion as well as acting as a contrast to the soft watercolour washes. The painting took two hours to complete, and I was pleased with the overall vitality of the finished result.

Improving Your Compositions

Composition is crucial to the ultimate success or failure of a landscape painting. It is important to spend a short while walking around the location, absorbing the scene until you have found something that appeals to you enough to get started.

The use of a viewfinder at this point can be vital in narrowing the field of vision and creating the right composition. It also helps in deciding on what format is best for the purpose: landscape, portrait or square. Shown here is my simple viewfinder, made out of a stout card measuring 11 x 13cm (4¼ x 5⅛in), out of the middle of which I have cut an aperture of 3 x 4cm (1⅛ x 1⅝in). I have painted a five-tone scale down one side using black ink, adding water to it for the mid tones; this can be done with a soft graphite pencil. It can be helpful to look at the scene through half-closed eyes, as this helps to block out detail and see the main elements and tonal values; and working *contre-jour*, against the light, can also simplify the scene.

This thumbnail sketch was done with a ballpoint pen in a small hardback sketchbook. Time spent doing this is never wasted, as it can sort out vital priorities.

Think carefully about your subject and how its main shapes are to be arranged. Ideally there should be some interaction between the shapes, creating a sense of movement round the picture and, in most landscapes, a feeling of depth.

Aim for a contrast of shapes rather than shapes of a similar size and form. Horizontals and verticals are known to produce a tranquil feel in compositions, while diagonals create more energy and movement. Remember that the composition is not only about the positive elements of the painting, but equally about the negative spaces around the main shapes of the subject.

An important consideration in any landscape is the proportion of space devoted to land and sky and whether you choose a high or low horizon. Most artists base their compositions on the Golden Section, or Rule of Thirds as it is sometimes called. This is where points of interest are placed on the intersection of imaginary lines that divide the picture plane into thirds. Often these focal points may be narrative, or where the strongest contrast or colour is situated.

Lerryn

Lerryn is one of my favourite haunts in Cornwall, and contains some of the problems you will be faced with. Like the photograph, our eyes take in a broad view, so we tend to take in everything we see. From one spot there are many options and permutations in every scene; below are three examples, where I have arranged the same elements within portrait, landscape and square formats.

Square format

Here the emphasis is on the background and sky, so I lowered the horizon line. Because the boats here are all evenly spaced across the scene, I moved the two on the left so that they were slightly closer together. Good composition is as much about knowing what to leave out as it is deciding how to arrange what to put in.

Portrait format

Here the emphasis is on the foreground, so I moved the horizon line higher and placed the main boat as the focal point in the Golden Section.
I used a gentle and meandering 'S'-shape design, with the tide pool leading the eye to the main boat. This helps to create an interesting pattern of shapes and tones within the picture area.

Landscape format

Here the horizon line is raised slightly above the centre to avoid the picture being equally spaced. I cropped the boats on the left in order to focus the viewer's eye to the main boat: this not only creates a sense of space and intrigue, but also hints at there being more outside the picture.

Old Mill Creek
Watercolour

The subject matter of this painting contains many of the elements that inspire me, in particular my response to capturing water, atmosphere and light. My inspiration here was the hazy sunlight as it shimmered on the water and wet mudbanks; this contrasted with the strong, dark reflections from the trees and made for an exciting subject.

Reference Sketch
Felt-tip pen and charcoal • 25 x 30cm (10 x 12in)

materials

- 300gsm (140lb) Whatman Not prestretched paper
- 4B pencil
- Masking fluid
- Brushes: 2.5cm (1in) hake; Nos 14, 8, 4 and 3 round; 1.3cm (½in) filbert; No. 1 rigger
- Watercolours: cadmium orange; Naples yellow; permanent rose; cerulean blue; phthalo blue (red shade); raw sienna; burnt umber; cadmium red; viridian
- Gouache: white

1 Guided by my monochrome sketch, I sketched out the initial drawing in pencil and applied masking tape around the edge of the picture to act as a mount.

2 I applied masking fluid with an old brush to reserve the highlights, lightly picking up the tooth of the paper and spattering in the bottom left-hand corner. I used a ruler as an aid to create straighter lines, and let everything dry thoroughly, using a hairdryer to speed up the process.

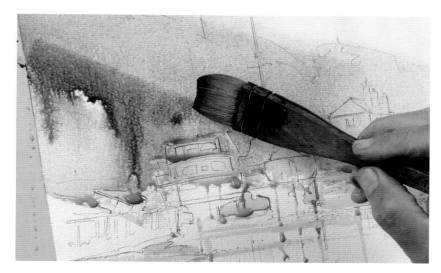

3 With a hake brush I lightly swept a mix of cadmium orange and Naples yellow over the top of the picture, varying the amount of water in the wash as I added more colour. While this was wet, I dropped in a mix of permanent rose and cerulean at the base of the sky, and then a darker mix of phthalo blue and raw sienna.

4 I carried on down the paper with combinations of the washes, blending and diluting the colours and leaving some parts of the paper white for highlights. To dry off excess runs I blotted the water with a piece of tissue paper. The initial base tones were now established, most of the white paper had been knocked back, and the soft mood was suggested with a range of warm and cool colours.

5 Making sure everything was completely dry, I now applied a little masking fluid over some of the initial washes – along the roofs of the buildings, along the bridge and at the side of the house – to reserve them while I applied more colour. I then built up the sky with more cerulean/rose washes, working lightly, then added warmth with the orange/yellow wash while wet. To build up the tones further, I used sweeping strokes across the paper and alternated between the washes, finishing with more blue/sienna for the darker areas.

6 When these washes were completely dry I mixed up some strong dark washes from burnt umber, cadmium red and phthalo blue; with a No. 14 round brush I started on the left-hand boat, varying the mix as I worked towards the right-hand hull, where I brought in more red and brought this down into its reflection in the water.

7 As I built up the washes going down to the water I tried to keep everything simple and uncomplicated. I applied a darkish mix of phthalo blue, raw sienna and burnt umber for the foreground water, working wet-into-wet from left to right.

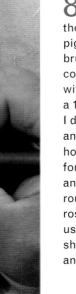

8 (See left) I applied more dark brown washes to the left-hand trees and those above the buildings, pulling the pigment around with clean water on the brush to soften the edges and blend the colours. For the reflections, I started with an orange/yellow mix applied with a 1.3cm (½in) filbert brush, into which I dropped a dark mix of burnt umber and phthalo blue, using vertical and horizontal brushstrokes; for the middle foreground I used a mix of cerulean blue and permanent rose. Switching to a No. 8 round brush, I used the cerulean blue/rose mix to tint the hulls of the boats. I used the same mix for the wall and its shadow on the shore, behind the house and a few touches for the windows.

Assessment

After checking that the entire picture was dry, I removed the masking tape, rubbed off the masking fluid and stood back to check my progress. The basic painting was now in place. With the white of the paper reinstated, I found the area in the middle distance indistinct and not really placed compared to the sky and foreground – by now it should have looked like a reflective surface of water, and thus needed attention. I also wanted to tie it all together in terms of tone and colour.

9 To give some hint of distance I applied a very pale, diluted wash of cerulean blue and permanent rose, then used this to knock back the roofs, chimneys and sides of the buildings as a glaze, just leaving a suggestion of light there. Again using the ruler as a mahlstick, I then applied the same mix to some of the white area below the bridge.

10 By continuing to knock back the white paper – but not all of it – I began to see some unity in the painting. I applied cerulean blue around the boats to knock back the coolness of the greens.

11 Moving back to the left-hand trees, I darkened the areas around them with a mix of raw sienna and cerulean blue with the side of the brush to get a wideish stroke and show the tooth of the paper. I then used the brush tip to bring the pigment down into the edges of the building. I did the same on the right, having wetted the paper first to be able to work wet-in-wet.

12 To bring further unity to the picture I carried on with the same mix in the water – the dark reflections of the boats were very important to the overall feel, so I took time to get the right tones and colours. I used a No. 4 round brush for the dinghy on the left, then added the dark for the arches of the bridge and below the keels of the boats.

13 Using a No. 4 round brush, I applied horizontal drybrush strokes with a dry mix of raw sienna and burnt umber, softening some parts of this with clean water. I used the same technique on the water in the middle distance to achieve some dappling of light. In the bottom left, I used a cerulean blue/rose mix to knock back more white areas and add form through shadows. After placing a touch of red to the keel to make the right-hand boat the focal point, I used a mix of cerulean blue and Naples yellow for the cool green of the land going into the water.

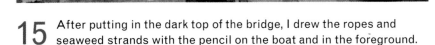

14 (Above) I made a strongish mix of viridian and a little cerulean blue for the canopy of the right-hand boat, and then added the reflections of this in the water. I added a diluted wash of cerulean blue and permanent rose to the mill and bridge to bring in more colour and form. Now I was on the home straight – if you're still looking for things to do at this stage, this suggests you're nearly there! I tightened up the shapes over all the picture where these were needed and put some more form into the bridge.

15 After putting in the dark top of the bridge, I drew the ropes and seaweed strands with the pencil on the boat and in the foreground.

16 To finish I applied some white gouache below the bridge and boat, dragging the brush almost dry across the paper. Using a No. 1 rigger brush and a ruler I applied a mix of white gouache and a little cerulean blue and cadmium red for the boat details and mast, continuing the latter with a dark red/blue mix. A few flicks with the rigger brush for the seagulls completed the painting.

TIPS

- Always keep your water jar full, then you can gauge easily just how far the brush is being immersed and hence how much water it will hold.

- Use large brushes as much as possible to avoid fiddling too early in your painting.

- Don't overfill your painting – keep a restful area somewhere in your work.

Finished Painting
Old Mill Creek
Watercolour
30 x 39cm (12 x 15½in)

My objective was to draw out the character of the place and capture the soft, hazy light and the tranquillity of the scene. I did this by limiting the colour range and using the translucency of watercolour, striving to put the colour on as simply as possible and keeping the washes light and alive without overworking – for example, the deep reflections in the river had to be dark but at the same time translucent and reflective.

Sunlit Creek, Porth Navas
Watercolour and pastel
36 x 53cm (14 x 21in)
*I find wooded tidal creeks such as this are full of mood
and atmosphere. Here the reserved highlights of the paper
contrasted well with the wet-in-wet washes of watercolour
and textures created by the pastel.*

Summer Haze, Dartmouth
Watercolour
13 x 36cm (5 x 14in)

Mist rising from the river and a soft hazy light were the inspiration for this painting, and watercolour was the perfect choice for capturing it.

Wet Mud
Watercolour
13 x 18cm (5 x 7in)

From a busy scene I selected two boats, but it was the colours in the wet mud that were my main interest behind this small watercolour. I used layered washes of watercolour as well as the wet-in-wet technique for capturing this.

Morning Light, Lerryn
Pastel
36 x 53cm (14 x 21in)
I painted this plein air pastel as a demonstration to students on a painting course in Cornwall, and had to compose the subject carefully as it was a complex scene. Remember that you are the picture-maker and don't have to record everything that you see.

Dappled Light, River Tone
Oils
36 x 36cm (14 x 14in)
My first consideration here was to establish the sunlit and shadow areas early on, as these would be constantly changing. The colour of the stained board was allowed to show through and acted as an important unifying element in the finished painting.

CHAPTER FIVE

Trees and Buildings

Autumn Sunshine
Oils
25 x 36cm (10 x 14in)
I wanted to convey the contrast of the autumn sunlight with its dappled shadows in this picture.

'We see nothing till we truly understand it.'

JOHN CONSTABLE

For every landscape painter trees and buildings form an irresistible and indispensable part of the picture-making process. Whether a classic view of a church or farm, nestling in the open countryside, or a more intimate scene, such as the interior of a dense wood, the subject has much to offer. Although not appropriate in every landscape, buildings, figures and animals not only add a narrative element, but can also bring a scene to life. They may not be the centre of interest; in my own paintings, they usually play a supporting role rather than a major one.

That said, for many artists trees and buildings have been the main passion: this was certainly the case for two latter-

day watercolour painters, Edward Wesson and Rowland Hilder. I have always admired their individual approach in tackling the landscape and in particular trees and buildings: the freshness of Wesson's watercolours and line and wash drawings, done in ink with a matchstick or sharpened lollipop stick, and Hilder with his distinctive approach to the subject, especially those paintings that depict the Kent landscape in winter. They were two totally contrasting painters, the first a 'purist' in watercolour, while for the other there were no rules in painting. You may also find it worthwhile to study them further, as you can learn a great deal from these masters of their craft.

Long Sutton from Muchelney
Felt-tip pen and charcoal
41 x 28cm (16 x 11in)

Otter Estuary
Pencil
27 x 36cm (10½ x 14in)

The sketchbook

Sketching buildings is often about gathering detailed information from the scene. These carefully rendered drawings are done in ballpoint, fibre-tip pen or graphite pencil. Adding watercolour to line drawings is well suited with buildings, particularly for textures.

To simplify a complicated scene or create atmosphere, I use a broader medium, such as fibre-tip pen and charcoal. Charcoal also works well when watercolour washes are laid over it, as these move the charcoal around giving it a granular and gritty quality.

When it comes to trees, practise drawing trees singly to begin with, as any weaknesses show up immediately when you include groups of trees in a composition. For measuring and checking shapes and proportions, I use the pencil and thumb technique, as shown on page 105. For a broader treatment of trees, I like to use fibre-tip pens and charcoal.

Bicton Farm from Otterton
Felt-tip pen, charcoal and conté crayon
38 x 28cm (15 x 11in)
Sketching buildings is often about gathering detailed information from a scene to use as an aide-memoire *in the studio.*

Choosing a medium

Trees and buildings can present a number of problems to the artist, in particular simplifying a subject that contains much detail.

Pastel is ideal for painting trees, as there is no colour mixing required – this means you can put the colour on directly, as long as you have a good range of greens to choose from. A range of softer warm and cool greens as well as brown-greens is useful for a northern landscape, whereas brighter greens may be needed for painting in the Mediterranean.

Pastel applied on its side is perfect for creating foliage masses and suggesting the form, shapes and texture of both winter and summer trees. The broken colour of pastel strokes can also be a perfect solution in suggesting texture in buildings simply, without getting too detailed.

For painting trees in watercolour, a large round or filbert brush is ideal for creating summer foliage, and a rigger brush is indispensable for painting fine branches and twigs.

Painting trees and buildings

It is a good idea to begin drawing trees in winter, when their construction and basic shapes are visible. During the summer months the profusion of green, with little variation of colour, can cause problems.

Assess the colours in trees, noting in particular the effects of aerial perspective. Bark colours are not just brown, but have a wonderful array of subtle colours.

Observe the general shape of the trunk and branches in silhouette, seeing it simply and clearly as a pattern of shapes and tone.

Trees must also give the impression of being firmly rooted in the ground; shadows can help describe the form and geometry of the landscape, as well as giving form to the trees.

When drawing buildings, a basic knowledge of the principals of linear perspective is important. One of the main rudiments is that all lines above your eye level come down to a vanishing point on the horizon line; similarly, all the lines below eye level appear to slant upwards to the focal point.

Towards Roddino, Piemonte
Pastel
43 x 34cm (17 x 13in)
In the heat of summer in the mountains of northern Italy the colourful features of the landscape tend to dominate the cloudless skies, so choosing a high horizon line can become necessary.

Glastonbury Tor
Watercolour and pastel
36 x 46cm (14 x 18in)
Pastel applied on its side is perfect for creating the impression of foliage masses and suggesting the form, shapes and texture of trees both in winter and summer.

Creating the Illusion of Depth and Space

Creating space and depth is one of the main challenges in a landscape painting, and can be a daunting prospect. Depth and recession in a painting can be created in a number of ways, using both linear and atmospheric perspective.

Linear perspective is based on three factors: viewpoint, horizon and vanishing point. A simple rule of linear perspective dictates that parallel horizontal lines, such as a road, converge at a vanishing point on the horizon. The eye tends to 'read' a picture from left to right; therefore it is useful to lead the eye purposely into a scene by way of a path or ploughed field, for instance.

Overlapping shapes also create the illusion of depth, such as a view of mountains that recede into the distance. This can be increased further when combined with differences of size, such as a row of trees. Placing the horizon line either high or low on the paper also has the effect of creating a dramatic sense of space.

The most important way of creating depth is the use of colour and tones in the painting, known as aerial or atmospheric perspective. This effect is caused by the presence of dust and moisture particles in the air, which make shapes greyer and less distinct the further away they are. The main principles of atmospheric perspective are simply that paler or cooler colours tend to recede, and darker or warmer colours tend to advance – the closer the object, the more colourful and distinct it is.

The effect of aerial perspective varies with the light conditions and where you are in the world, of course. In my travels in northern Italy, for instance, the clear harsh light enabled me to see great vistas in every direction; in situations like this, you have to sometimes exaggerate aerial perspective in order to achieve a feeling of depth. In different parts of the world, on the other hand, the light and atmosphere may be much softer and more subdued.

Vineyards near Alba, Northern Italy
Pastels
53 x 35.5cm (21 x 14in)
The main elements of aerial perspective are evident in this painting and contribute to an overall sense of space and depth.

In the distance the tonal contrasts lessen, the textures soften and the colours become much cooler and bluer.

In the middle distance perspective tells the viewer that the rows of vines close up as they recede. A cooler blue has been added to accentuate this.

Here the warm ochre colour of the tinted pastel paper has been retained for the foreground and so advances. Stronger tones and texture have been added than elsewhere in the painting.

JULY 2000

Cissone, Piemonte, Italy

Sensation

When my good friend and fellow artist Alan Cotton asked me to lead a painting group to the hills of the Langhe in northern Italy, I knew that it would be a memorable experience. The light governs the character of a place, and the intense colours and vibrant clear skies brought the features of the landscape into sharp focus. Here the clarity of the far-reaching vistas was laid bare and demanded to be painted. The regimented rows of green vines provided wonderful patterns over the yellow ochre earth, and the bright red roofs of the hilltop villages broke up the landscape with splashes of vibrant colour.

The media I find best suited for subjects like this are oils or pastels. Pastels are particularly convenient when travelling abroad, as they are very portable.

I soon found that early morning and early evening were the best times to paint, not only because the temperatures were more bearable but also because the light was far more inspiring. The evening light was particularly dramatic, with its intensity of colour and tonal depth, the shapes in the landscape beautifully linked by the long cast shadows. The mood and atmosphere also intensified with these extremes. This painting, however, was done in the searing heat of the day, so the first priority was to find a view under shade.

The elevated village of Roddino is typical of the many views to be found in this area, and stands proudly overlooking its cultivated fields and wooded slopes.

Process

For this painting I combined watercolour and pastel and used my viewfinder to decide on a suitable format – I decided on a portrait view, as it was the dappled light and shade in the foreground that I found inspiring.

On a sheet of 400gsm (200lb) Bockingford watercolour paper I sketched in the scene with a waterproof fibre-tip pen. I next laid in an overall wash of cadmium orange and Winsor blue for the foundation, leaving some areas

of the white paper showing for the highlights, in particular the sunlit areas of the path. It is difficult to paint with pastel on white paper because the colours always appear brighter, so I always work on a mid-tone foundation of either paint or a mid-tone pastel paper – glare on a white sheet of paper can be very difficult, particularly in strong light like this.

The photograph above shows me painting the view of Roddino from Cissone, shown in the photograph below.

Sarravalle Langhe from Cissone
Felt-tip pen and charcoal
36 x 28cm (14 x 11in)
The tonal value sketch of a scene is more important to a painting's success than getting the colours right.

**Roddino
from Cissone,
Piemonte**
Watercolour and pastel
53 x 36cm (21 x 14in)
*The mood of the
finished painting
is determined by
using the princi-
ples of aerial per-
spective, making
the distance cooler
and the foreground
both warmer and
darker.*

Mountain Village
Pastels

The Isle of Arran in Scotland is full of breathtaking subjects for the painter, but it was the stunning location of Lochranza in the north of the island that I returned to for many of my subjects on a recent trip. The village lies within a sheltered bay with its distinctive cottages set against a backcloth of towering majestic mountains, and is a captivating subject for any landscape painter.

I used a small pen and watercolour sketch as a reference, and used soft pastel for this demonstration, as it was all about powerful contrasts and visual richness of colour.

Seeing the scene against the light also helped me to simplify the scene and create the dramatic mood required for the painting.

materials

- Arches 140lb (300gsm) Not prestretched paper
- Acrylic: raw umber
- Pastels: pale blue, white-blue, light purple-grey, off white, dark purple-grey, mid purple-grey, light green-grey, mid green-grey, dark green-grey, dark olive green, dark Hooker's green, dark sap green, mid sap green, lizard green, mid blue-grey, pale pink, pink-grey, dark purple-brown, dark green, olive green, pale sage green, dark brown, dark blue-grey, dark red-brown
- Pastel pencils: light grey, dark blue-purple, purple
- Black permanent chisel-tip marker pen
- Conté sticks: black, white
- Paper tissue
- Safety razor blade

Reference Sketch
Pen and watercolour
13 x 18cm (5 x 7in)

1 I started with an acrylic base of raw umber, leaving a sweep of paper unstained to catch the sparkle of the loch water. When this was dry I made the initial drawing with a black permanent chisel-tip marker pen.

2 Starting with the sky, I covered much of the paper with strokes made using the sides of pastels: pale blue, whiter blue, light purple-grey and off white. To solidify certain areas and take off some of the toothed texture, I smoothed the pastel marks using my fingers, the side of my hand and paper tissue.

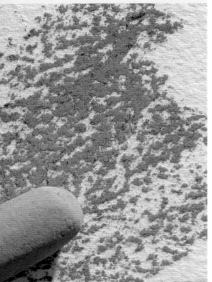

3 While these colours were in my hand I looked to see where else they could be used, and echoed the sky in the water. This time I didn't blend the colours but dragged them across the paper to pick up the tooth (all except the off white) to preserve the water's sparkle.

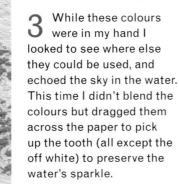

4 I started the hills with a dark purple-grey to establish a base with the brown acrylic support. I then added other shades of purple-grey and a variety of green-greys as I moved from the left to the right, working darkest along the ridges to form a hard edge with the sky.

5 As I built up the tonal range of the hills, I began to blend the pastel marks with fingers and tissue, making sure to leave the brown base showing through in parts. Where the pastel was the wrong colour, I lifted this off with the side of a safety razor blade, in order to apply a new colour without clogging up the paper; a hoghair brush can also be used to lift off pastel.

6 Working through the range of colours, I went over the whole picture strengthening crucial edges, particularly in the middle-distance hills and in front of the distant left-hand hill.

7 To fix the trees and scrubby bushes I applied dark olive green, dark Hooker's green and darker green-grey, then added lighter areas of foliage with a dark sap green and a mid sap green, bringing these down and to the right.

8 The essence of this picture is the play of light across it; to catch the light at the tops of the trees I used a very bright lizard green, and enhanced this by drawing blue-grey around the trees, using them as negative shapes. Staying with the blue-grey, I moved into the water area, making downward strokes with the pastel stick.

9 I started the road, moving horizontally across the picture and then coming down on the right side with a very pale pink, and reinforced this with the purple-grey used to start the hills; a little blending was required, but not too much. I also used the purple-grey on the right side of the shore and the shadow sides of the buildings, then built up the shore with darker pink-greys.

10 While building up and warming the shadow sides of the buildings with deep purple-brown, I was careful to keep the strokes and marks simple and uncomplex. I used dark green and olive green to suggest shadows in the right-hand bank, and dark green for the trees and hedges at the foot of the hills and around the buildings, then reflected these colours in the water. Pale sage green was useful for foreshore highlights.

11 For the lighter parts of the buildings I used a pale purple-grey. This same colour was then stroked into the water blending the colours with fingers and tissue; I worked vertically first, then added horizontal strokes.

12 After using the pale purple-grey on the other buildings, I applied the same colour to the road in front. For the parts of the tree foliage in deepest shadow I used a very dark brown to contrast with the palest greens, and deepened this a little with a black conté stick. To highlight the sunlit areas of the main building, I used the tip of a white conté stick (see above).

Assessment

I removed the masking tape and stood back to view my progress. At this point I felt that the middle distance, in front of the left-hand hill, needed blending, and that all the hills could use more contour work, but not so much that they dominated the scene. Remembering the direction of the light was vital at all times.

13 (Left) A cool green-grey pastel was used to achieve the contours in the hills, as well as create a sense of depth to the scene.

14 Going back into the water with a dark blue-grey and a lighter purple-grey, I used big horizontal strokes to catch the tooth of the white paper and allow the sparkle to show through. I also brought in the light blue of the sky here, lightening the stroke as the sky colour met the foreshore.

15 After darkening the left-hand buildings a little with dark purple-grey, I added off-white highlights on the tops of the walls and buildings. I now switched to pastel pencils: a light grey unified the roofs, and a dark blue-purple added the angles on the buildings. I pulled the light grey pencil across the water for shallow highlit areas. For the tree branches and trunks I used a deep red-brown pastel stick, and brought some of this colour into the wall.

16 With the full range of pastels I enhanced contrasts by drawing negative shapes and finding contrasts. I made dots on the water to enhance the sparkle, and stroked more pale blue over the edge of the foreshore. To finish, I used a purple pencil to enhance the shadows, and reinforced edges and angles across the picture.

Finished Painting
Mountain Village
Pastel
34 x 42cm (13½ x 16½in)
*My main aim was to set out and achieve
a strong contrast and mood in this painting.
Choosing a warm mid-tone background
helped complement the blues and greens
put on with pastel. This not only created a
vibration of colour where the edges met and
the tone came through, but also helped to
unify the whole painting.*

TIPS
• Make sure to keep a reference chart of your
  colours, as it makes re-ordering much easier.

• The main problem with pastels is getting
  too many colours going too fast, so keep
  the pastels you use separate. This will help
  restrict you to a more limited palette.

(Opposite)
Near Leenaun, Connemara
Pastel
51 x 36cm (20 x 14in))
The cottages nestling on the steep slopes of the mountainside and grouped around a pretty bridge caught my eye immediately. Finding the traditional haystacks here too, made the scene even more appealing.

Reflections, Lochranza Castle, Isle of Arran
Oils
36 x 36cm (14 x 14in))
In this painting I made use of the surface of the prepared gesso board with thinly applied paint helping to suggest texture in the castle walls. The highlights and details in the walls were then lifted out with a rag and a sharpened end of a brush handle.

Rainclouds over Lower Coombe Farm
Oils
25 x 36cm (10 x 14in)
I love it when buildings, trees and fields are lit up against the backdrop of a dramatic sky. The richness of oils lends itself beautifully to painting subjects such as this.

(Opposite above)

Summer Fields, Ashcombe
Oils
25 x 36cm (10 x 14in)
Be sure to pay attention to negative shapes in a painting. Here the shapes of the sky and fields describe the rhythm and gesture of the trees, which makes it easier to create more interesting positive shapes.

(Opposite below)

Reflections, Bridge Inn, Topsham
Watercolour and pastel
33 x 45cm (13 x 18in)
Soft pastel is particularly useful in suggesting texture on buildings. Here a pastel was used lightly on its side to suggest the stonework in the bridge without getting into too much detail.

Golden Summer, Powderham
Watercolour and pastel
34 x 41cm (13 x 16in)
The illusion of depth is created here by the round hay bales, which not only overlap but also reduce in size as they recede. The depth is further enhanced by the warm, rich foreground shadows.

CHAPTER SIX

Moorland, Mountains and Waterfalls

'Paint generously and unhesitatingly, for it is better not to lose the first impression.'

CAMILLE PISSARRO

Pen-y-Pass, Snowdon
Pastel on tinted pastel paper
37 x 55cm (14½ x 21½in)
This scene involved blending pastel as well as using firmer, more direct marks that affect the ridges of the mountains.

Moorland, mountains and waterfalls have long been a source of inspiration for many fine painters. Changing weather can be frustrating for the painter, but in this environment, the many varying moods are its main attraction: somehow these landscapes lend themselves to brooding atmospheres of storms or mist and many other transient elements. Although the artist is very much exposed to these, bad weather can often be seen gathering some distance away, so at least you can prepare for it.

Water plays an important role here, as in its many forms it imparts life to these landscapes – whether it is a cascading waterfall or a still, reflective loch, few artists can resist the subject.

Waterfall, Glen Rosa, Isle of Arran
Ballpoint, watersoluble felt-tip pen and pencil
13 x 17cm (5 x 6½in)
Watersoluble pens and pencils are invaluable for quick sketches, particularly in more remote places. Tonal values can be applied with minimum equipment to suggest the patterns of light and shade in the landscape.

Choosing a medium

For these subjects I prefer to use oils, pastels or mixed media (watercolour and pastels combined), as these media's strong tones and depth of colour are more suitable for capturing the mood, atmosphere and grandeur of moorlands, mountains and waterfalls.

Painting in watercolour does not convey this intangible quality for me unless it is combined with pastel. Working on a tinted support with pastels or oils adds to this overall depth: a dark paper shows the pastels as brighter, but the overall tonality is dark, while the mid-tone range matches most colours and intensifies the brilliance of colour.

By matching the overall tonality of your paper to suit the subject you can achieve the maximum luminosity from your pastels. I sometimes tint watercolour paper with a number of flat washes to create my own coloured supports. When working in watercolour and pastel combined I work mainly on watercolour paper, particularly making use of the whiteness of the paper if the scene has a lighter sky or a waterfall, for instance.

Working on a coloured ground in oils quickly establishes the tonal range, particularly if a dark and light are stated early in the painting.

The sketchbook

Many of my waterfall paintings have had to be done in the studio from sketches and photographs simply because of the remoteness of the subject. Although conditions may sometimes be difficult, combining sketching with walking can be thoroughly enjoyable, as to explore all its hidden secrets and understand this subject fully, it has to touch all your senses.

In these situations, where much walking is needed, travelling light is an important factor, and materials should be restricted to what will fit into a backpack; for me, these usually consist of quick sketches done in pencil or pens, including ballpoint, permanent fibre-tip or watersoluble, in a small hardback sketchbook. I sometimes add colour with washes of watercolour. These drawings tend to record topographical features rather than mood and atmosphere. This is best captured in a broader medium: charcoal is ideally suited, as the composition and large masses can be produced extremely quickly in a painterly fashion.

Hay Tor, Dartmoor
Felt-tip pen and graphite pencil
13 x 17cm (5 x 6½in)
In this sketch I combined felt-tip pen with a soft graphite pencil to help achieve tonal contrast and distance.

Sunset, Twelve Bens, Connemara
Conté crayon and charcoal
25 x 36cm (10 x 14in)
I often add written notes to remind me of the colours when back in the studio.

Painting moorland, mountains and waterfalls

Mountains and moorlands present a number of problems, the main one being scale: the vastness of the scene can be overwhelming. Most landscapes are painted in a horizontal, landscape format, but a portrait view can work better here. There must be a foreground, for without this it is impossible to appreciate the scale and majesty of a mountainous background. We actually see more detail in a foreground, but it is better to simplify this; I often take up a lower eye level and look through grasses to make the scene more interesting.

Focus on shapes, not things, and think of your paintings as mosaics of interlocking shapes, some larger, some smaller, but all related. In a mountain scene there are a number of main lines formed by mountainsides and foreground slopes. If these lines are continued, the majority will meet at one or more points; these are the vanishing points, and general composition depends on their position.

The simplest composition is one where there is only one vanishing point, and in this case it is best for it to lie outside, instead of inside, the picture area. This means that the eye is led out of the picture area and wants to suggest more. You may find it useful to give some idea of the true size of a mountain by including a farmhouse, animals, or trees for instance.

Clouds both beautify any scene and add a sense of scale and distance. It is important to work quickly and also organize the arrangement of the sky in the painting from the outset – and then keep to it. Shadows are a useful aid to composition, particularly morning or evening shadows as they steal across the landscape and change it.

Mountains and water – the two are synonymous, and waterfalls, rivers and lakes impart life to a landscape. Few artists can resist painting the subject, yet the bubbling, dashing turbulence is often transformed into something static and lifeless in paint. Simplifying and working with speed are my tips for success. I also find that a broad treatment, with any medium, will carry more conviction, particularly when painting moving water.

Moorland Falls, Dartmoor
Watercolour and pastel
45 x 48cm (18 x 19in)
Moving water is best treated as simply as possible, for once it becomes too detailed all the flowing movement seems to be lost.

Ashleagh Falls, County Mayo
Watercolour and pastel
36 x 53cm (14 x 21in))
Set in a truly spectacular location, these falls had all the ingredients for a painting to be painted in watercolour and pastel.

Mixing Realistic Greens

Colour is a personal thing, and no two painters see the same colour in a scene. There are hundreds of different shades in nature's greens, which, if followed exactly, would result in pictorial cacophony. Sometimes colours in nature, especially local ones, if matched exactly, can strike a discordant note in your colour scheme too.

For each medium it is worth making a colour chart showing mixes obtained from various blues and yellows. Adding any warm colour to this mix will extend the range further. Such a chart will not only familiarize you with the various mixes, but also provide a useful reference guide for the future.

Yellow influences the nature of the green more than blue does, so if you want a sharp, cool green, for instance, use a cool yellow such as lemon yellow. If you want a warm green, use a warm yellow such as cadmium yellow.

Many watercolour manufacturers produce greens that are 'acid' in colour; these harsher greens can be modified with the addition of a warmer colour, as shown below in watercolour, where cadmium red and raw umber modify the harsh bought green.

Each colour has a warm or cool bias; here are examples of greens mixed from ultramarine blue (warm) with cadmium yellow (warm) and lemon yellow (cool).

Harmonious colour mixing: adding red to green modifies it and makes a warmer and more subtle colour.

Painting in pastel is much easier, as there is no or little colour mixing needed; you simply choose the right colour you need for the scene. You do not need a huge range, but it is important that you have a dark, medium and light of various warm and cool shades. Manufacturers supply hand-coloured charts of colours, but you have to pay for them. If you do need to mix a colour with pastels, always put the lighter colour down first, as putting a lighter one over a darker one rarely works.

Most landscapes can be painted with the limited palette of greens shown here.

Lough Corrib, Connemara
Oils
35 x 35cm (14 x 14in)
Mixing warm and cool yellows and red with viridian produced the wide range of greens needed in the foreground of this painting.

Viridian is the base of all true green pigment; in oils I use it as my main green, adding red to darken and yellow to lighten it.

Dolwyddelan, Snowdonia, North Wales

Sensation

When I was asked to run a painting course in the heart of Snowdonia, I jumped at the chance, as this was somewhere I had never painted before. However, mixed with the sense of excitement was a sense of awe at the prospect. To familiarize ourselves with the scenery, on the first day we walked up the hill a short distance from the studio and looked back down towards the village of Dolwyddelan. It was a sunny morning with a fresh breeze and some cloud. First, I encouraged my students to sketch in monochrome before I did my demonstration. It was important to ease them into the subject – and myself too, for that matter!

The mountain Moel Siabod dwarfs the village, and in the far distance we could see Snowdon – the highest mountain in the National Park. There were many challenges to be faced in painting this scene, most notably the sheer scale of the subject, as well as the overall greenness of the scene.

When painting any landscape, the first consideration is to establish the main interest: whether it is the landscape or the sky. Often views like this can take up to two-thirds of the picture area, so you need to consider the format: a square or portrait format may work better than a landscape shape.

It is always best to suggest grandeur simply, so I first produced a couple of quick sketches to sort out my main interest using a fibre-tip pen and charcoal. I particularly liked the way the drystone wall led one's eye into the scene to the cottage, and then beyond to Snowdon. I was also inspired about the strong contrasts of sun and shade, and in particular the way the roof and top of the wall had caught the light.

These photographs show the students sketching, as well as the chosen view for my painting. The bright sunlit roofs and the light catching the top of the wall were what initially inspired me.

Process

For this demonstration I used watercolour and pastels combined on Fabriano 140lb (300gsm) Not watercolour paper. I sketched the scene using a waterproof fibre-tip pen and applied masking fluid to reserve the highlights on the top of the wall and roof. I laid an overall wash of raw sienna, cadmium orange and Winsor

blue, working wet-in-wet for the sky. When this was dry I applied a further wash of these colours mixed together for the mountains and the landscape.

For the brighter green in the foreground I used aureolin with a touch of the blue, and then mixed the orange with the blue to produce the darks in the wall and shadow areas. It was important that the shadows were stated early on and adhered to until the end. I mixed sepia with Winsor blue for the darkest colour in

Snowdon from Dolwyddelan
Felt-tip pen and charcoal
25 x 36cm (10 x 14in)
Before starting the painting I produced this quick sketch to help me with the composition and tonal values.

Watercolour stage
Using a large hake brush I lay the watercolour foundation, concentrating more on contrast and shapes than trying to match the right colour.

the wall. When this was dry I rubbed the masking fluid off with my finger.

Because the summer greens were dominant, I decided to introduce more recession in the painting by introducing a range of cooler colours in the distance, using purple, grey and cool green pastels. I was careful not to cover all the watercolour, but instead balanced the two media together, the pastel acting as a catalyst for the watercolour by sparking off its vibrancy. The soft, transparent washes of watercolour and the hard opaque pastel marks can be seen to good effect here, particularly in the sky and foreground. I used warmer green/browns in the trees and some warmer red/browns in the wall.

Snowdon from Dolwyddelan
Watercolour and pastel   36 x 46cm (14 x 18in)
The mood and atmosphere of the finished painting were determined by exaggerating the rules of aerial perspective, in order to establish distance and depth.

Waterfall
Watercolour and pastels

Like many artists, I find myself drawn irresistibly to the evocative power, both in the sight and sound, of a tumbling waterfall. For this painting of a waterfall at Glen Rosa, I decided on combining two media together, watercolour and pastels. For reference I used a couple of sketches, one done in fibre-tip pen and charcoal and the other in pen and watercolour. I preferred the composition of the monochrome sketch, as it added more drama to the scene, so I mainly referred to this during the painting process.

Reference Sketches
(Above)
Felt-tip pen and charcoal
25 x 36cm (10 x 14in)
(Left)
Pen and watercolour
13 x 18cm (5 x 7in)

materials

- 4b graphite pencil
- 140lb (300gsm) Not Arches prestretched paper
- Black chisel-tip permanent fibre-tip pen
- Brushes: 2.5cm (1in) hake; No. 14 filbert; No. 8 round
- Masking fluid
- Watercolours: cadmium orange; Naples yellow; phthalo blue (red shade); raw sienna; burnt umber; permanent rose; cerulean blue; viridian
- Gouache: flesh tint; permanent white
- Pastels: light purple-grey, dark purple-grey, dark forest green, mid red-grey, dark red-grey, dark purple, light pink, light blue-grey, sage green. dark brown-red
- Conté stick: black
- Tissue

1 I sketched in the initial drawing using a permanent chisel-tip pen, as this would not be affected by subsequent watercolour washes and would not fill up the tooth of the paper. Placing the darkest darks early on also helped me establish the tonal range.

2 I began by flicking in some masking fluid to reserve the white paper for highlights, particularly in the waterfall; I applied the fluid quite lightly and dragged it across the paper, picking up the tooth of the watercolour paper.

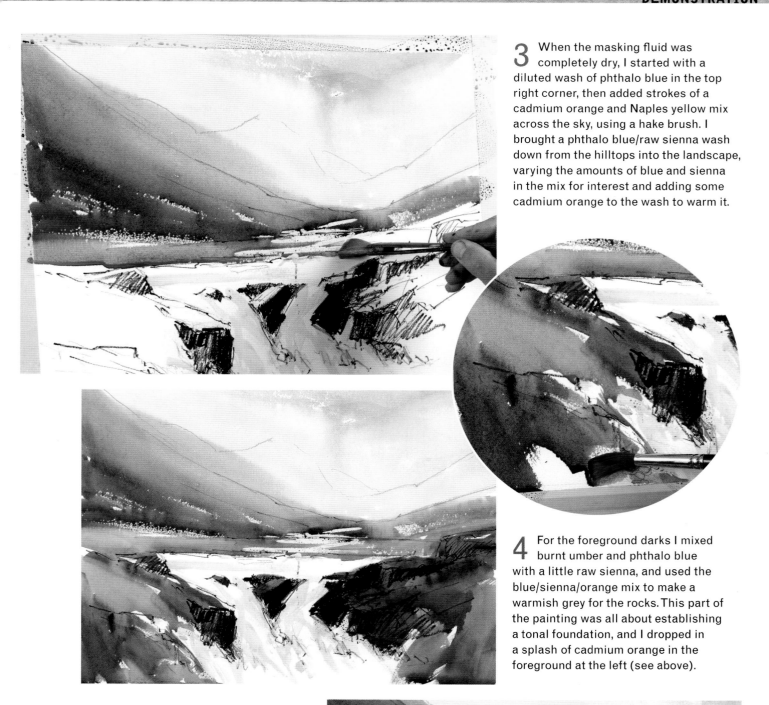

3 When the masking fluid was completely dry, I started with a diluted wash of phthalo blue in the top right corner, then added strokes of a cadmium orange and Naples yellow mix across the sky, using a hake brush. I brought a phthalo blue/raw sienna wash down from the hilltops into the landscape, varying the amounts of blue and sienna in the mix for interest and adding some cadmium orange to the wash to warm it.

4 For the foreground darks I mixed burnt umber and phthalo blue with a little raw sienna, and used the blue/sienna/orange mix to make a warmish grey for the rocks. This part of the painting was all about establishing a tonal foundation, and I dropped in a splash of cadmium orange in the foreground at the left (see above).

5 To put in the distant mountains I used a cooler mix of phthalo blue and cadmium orange than previously, adding a bit of raw sienna to lighten the tone where necessary. After dropping some straight blue into the sky, I went back to the mountains and used the side of the brush to apply a mix of blue and raw sienna to suggest scree on the mountain slopes; I added some orange to harmonize with the foreground warmth and bring the middle distance forward, allowing all the washes to dry completely.

6 To give some more unity to the picture I went back to the sky, starting by wetting some of this area with clean water. While this was wet I dropped a mix of permanent rose and cerulean blue into it, and then brought the very diluted wash down on to the mountainsides to blend them with the sky.

7 I brought the same wash down into the middle distance and the furthest stretches of water, using it as a unifying glaze while leaving some of the underlying washes visible. To indicate some form in the bottom right corner I did some contour modelling with the same mix.

8 Moving forwards in the water, I used a No. 14 filbert to apply a watery wash of cadmium orange and Naples yellow, which reflected the sky colour, as did a diluted version of the rose and cerulean blue mix; I paid attention to the white of the paper as well as the masked areas. At the bottom of the water I put in a watery wash of viridian and then the rose/cerulean blue wash. I scrubbed and dabbed excess pigment and water with a clean tissue.

Assessment

With the masking tape removed, the watercolour washes not only built up a strong tonal foundation but would also contrast or harmonize with the pastels that would be applied next, and would also help to define and refine the mountains and sky.

9 Starting in the sky, I used the side of a light purple-grey pastel stick, bringing this down on the mountains. I used a tissue to blend the pastel and take off enough dust to diffuse the colour, giving a suggestion of the mountain tops showing through low cloud.

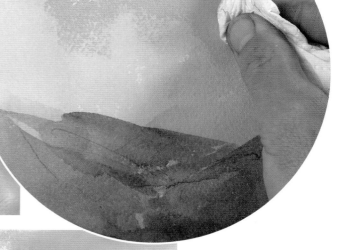

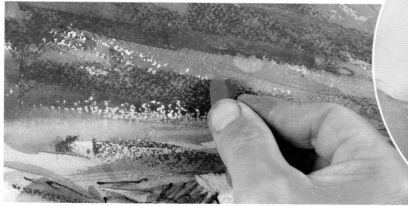

10 (Above) on the mountain slopes I used the side of a dark forest green pastel to catch the tooth of the paper, then used the same pastel to make rough, striking marks in the foreground – this is a rugged landscape, so I didn't want to make it pretty by tidying up the edges.

11 I dragged the same pastel I used for the sky across some of the white paper to show a still part of water, then switched to a darker purple-grey to darken parts of the central and right-hand mountains, leaving the watercolour washes to show up light. I then used the tip of the pastel to make a few tiny strokes and stripes in the foreground rocks, leaving the pastel unblended.

12 To put some form into the foreground rocks I went in quite strongly on the top edge with the side of a red-grey pastel, starting on the right and working across the central rock on to the left rocks. I then added the purple-grey of the sky into the water, making sure to leave white highlights.

13 Moving back to the rocks, I used a deep brown-red earth-colour pastel to put in the darks, this time working over the blackness of the marker pen (despite being labelled 'permanent', these pen marks will fade eventually). I then used a black conté stick to tighten up the darkest areas and provide more definition. I was not satisfied with the rocks, so created more edges, contours and form with a slightly darker red-grey pastel – I worked on top of the darkest shades with this, then added a darker purple to put in shadow areas and break up the other colours.

14 I added light purple-grey as reflections in the middle water, still leaving some white paper. To show the flow and direction of the water I brought the same colour into the foreground water, working very lightly to keep the sparkle in it. I then used a No. 8 round brush and an almost dry wash of burnt umber and phthalo blue to tighten up the rocks at their very darkest points.

15 With the same brush I lightened the rocks with flesh tint gouache. I then mixed white gouache with permanent rose and cerulean blue watercolours to make a lightish grey, and added further detail on all the foreground rocks.

16 When these new washes were completely dry, I used a light purple-grey pastel across the central rock to echo the sky colour and give more form to the rock. I reinforced this effect with a light, brighter pink and then went across the other rocks with a few flicks to further sharpen their definition. To finish, I pushed a light blue-grey pastel into the water and rocks, and used a sage green pastel to echo the colour of the mountains in the water.

Finished Painting
Waterfall
Watercolour and pastel
34 x 46cm (13½ x 18in)

There is a certain magic when you combine media in the same painting, as the results can sometimes be totally unexpected. However, it is also important to let each medium speak and make full use of its own qualities. This demonstration shows to good effect the interplay between a translucent medium and an opaque one, as well as many other contrasts achieved by using them together.

TIPS

- If you have a busy sky, keep the landscape simple, and vice versa.

- When painting water use expressive brushstrokes, which should always follow the flow of water.

Connemara Sky
Watercolour and pastel
36 x 53cm (14 x 21in)
Often you must search out a subject, but sometimes a scene finds you, as in this case. As I drove round a bend on the coast road to Clifden, the mountains, sea and sky seemed to encompass as one the true spirit of the place.

(Opposite)
Fairy Glen, Betws-y-Coed
Watercolour and pastel
51 x 41cm (20 x 16in)
Walking to Fairy Glen with all my equipment was difficult but well worth the effort. The glen has a mystical atmosphere, and after a few hours painting here I could almost feel the presence of the 'little creatures' playing on the rocks around me.

Dartmoor Sky
Watercolour and pastel
36 x 53cm (14 x 21in)
Here the late afternoon sun cast its long shadows across the summer landscape. This not only made for a more interesting composition but a more dramatic scene.

Towards Hay Tor, Dartmoor
Watercolour and pastel
33 x 40cm (13 x 16in)
I feel that a broad treatment of any subject can carry more conviction. This also applies to foregrounds; in order not to distract, here I have treated this simply, allowing the eye to pass into the picture easily.

Waterfall on the East Dart
Watercolour and pastel
36 x 53cm (14 x 21in)
Cascading waterfalls are an awe-inspiring sight, but capturing the spirit of moving water can be difficult. Here the pastel, along with the texture of the paper, was useful in describing the direction of movement, as well as simplifying the foam and bubbles.

Secret Waterfall, Snowdonia
Watercolour and pastel
36 x 43cm (14 x 17in)
This complex scene not only had to be carefully composed but also executed quickly, because of the constantly changing light and shadows. The highlights were reserved with masking fluid and the darks were stated early on in watercolour.

CHAPTER SEVEN

Seascapes

**Silver Sea,
Mawgan Porth**
Watercolour and pastel
33 x 43cm (13 x 17in)
*The sun breaking
through the clouds,
casting its strong light
on the sea, was my main
reason for choosing
this scene.*

'Still I should paint my own places best; painting is with me but another word for feeling.'
JOHN CONSTABLE

From thundering windswept waves crashing on to rugged rocks to the reflections of a golden sunset on a gentle swell – it is easy to understand the creative need to capture these emotional moments in paint.

The elemental forces in nature and the wide-open spaces of sea and sky have long been an inspiration in my work, just as for centuries the sea in all its many moods has inspired artists, poets and musicians alike.

I am also drawn to this exhilarating subject due to the fact that for the past two decades I have lived on the south coast of England, and such close proximity to the sea gives me endless variations on a theme. And once you get to the sea, you do not have to go far to find challenges new – although it is not far away in miles, I have always found the coast of Cornwall to the west to be a world away from my home of Devon in the fresh challenges it offers.

The sketchbook

Begin by sketching in monochrome using solid graphite pencils, watersoluble pens or pencils in a small hardback sketchbook. When your confidence has grown, work up to a larger A3 sketchbook using a broader medium such as charcoal sticks – this is a wonderfully expressive medium that lends itself beautifully to capturing the movement of waves, as broad tonal areas can be applied very quickly, as well as more sensitive line work. Waves and surf can be simply stated by lifting out with a putty eraser. Different effects can also be achieved by moving charcoal around with water.

Charcoal drawings also work well when watercolour washes are laid over, as this gives a granular quality that produces lovely textured areas. A combination of charcoal and white and black conté crayons on a tinted pastel paper can also produce exciting results.

The Quies from Treyarnon
Felt-tip pen and charcoal
25 x 30cm (10 x 12in)
The mood and atmosphere of crashing waves on a rugged coast can be caught beautifully with charcoal.

Choosing a medium

For me, to paint the power and dignity of the sea demands a medium with a directness of approach and a *bravura* technique – oils or mixed media (watercolour and pastels) are the perfect choices, as they give life and movement to the surface of paintings; particularly in oils the brushwork can express so much. Working quickly helps to create the excitement and energy, but keen observation and sound drawing must also back this up.

Constable's oil sketches present us with an intense encounter between the artist and the world about him. His evocative sketches not only record the facts but also his feelings in relation to them. They are sometimes controlled and descriptive, but are often wild, excited and inspired. Constable's sea paintings done at Brighton show us some of the wonderful fleeting effects of nature and his immediate response to them.

Pencil sketch
Making quick jottings in a small hardback sketchbook can be invaluable for under-standing the form, tones and colours found in rocks.

Between Showers, Mawgan Porth
Pencil and watercolour
18 x 53cm (7 x 21in)
Working across both pages of a hardback sketchbook is useful for recording skies, as well as the wide expanse of beach scenes.

Painting seascapes

Panoramic views of the open sea can present compositional difficulties. It is important therefore to create a focal point, even if there isn't one – some swirling seagulls, a sailing boat or a crashing wave, for instance.

There is a recession of colour and tone in waves just as there is in the landscape. They recede in tone from the lightest light in the foreground waves to those in the distance. If you hold up a small piece of white card to them, you will be able to identify this more easily.

Aerial perspective can enhance the feeling of distance, particularly with overlapping shapes and lighter tones, as shapes move back in space. The solidity and three-dimensional form of cliffs and rocks can be seen more clearly if you look for the main shapes by squinting at the scene, or by choosing a *contre-jour* view. They are also more dramatic on a sunny day, as the shadows and contrast help to emphasize the dignity and atmosphere of form and distance – shadows are not just black, but full of colour.

It also helps to think masses and larger shapes rather than detail: when painting in watercolour or oils, the essence of rock structures can often be best described by using a flat or filbert brush to achieve hard-edged, angular brushstrokes. No matter how interesting the colour may be, it won't help if your rocks lack form and solidity, so observe the

Sunset, Kilve
Oils
33 x 33cm (13 x 13in)
Skies produce vastly different light effects and colours on the sea, so the interaction between sea and sky must be an important consideration. For instance, a light sky makes the water look light, whereas a dark sky darkens the sea quite considerably.

tonal values of them carefully. When painting beaches, note how the colours and tones of the sand change as the waves recede – wet sand is initially light and reflective, but darkens as the water seeps away.

Beaches are always enlivened by the addition of figures, which give a feeling of movement and scale, and life to a picture – they also create a narrative in a picture as well as often contributing as a main focus of interest in a scene. Always make sure that your figures relate properly in size to their surroundings and are economically stated.

TIPS

• Pay special attention to negative shapes, the spaces around a subject. Working with negative shapes helps create more interesting positive shapes.

• When creating foam or spray in watercolour, try using a hard eraser to remove a little colour to create soft highlights. This is also perfect for suggesting shafts of sunlight in the sea.

Rinsey Cove
Watercolour and pastel
33 x 43cm (13 x 17in)
It is best to treat cliffs as simple shapes, and in this example 'less is more' applies admirably.

Interpreting Tones

Seeing and judging tones correctly is the key to any successful painting, and without this foundation a painting would soon collapse. The word 'tone' simply describes how dark or light an area is, whatever its colour, and half closing your eyes will help you to see the tonal masses in a scene.

Every colour has a tonal value from white to black, with an infinite range of greys in between. Compare the black-and-white reproduction shown on the right with the original painting, and you can see that some colours appear lighter, while others are darker; some, for instance red and green, appear similar in tone.

Although many artists work with a scale of nine to twelve tones, I recommend that you keep it simple by restricting yourself to five tones to begin with. A tone scale such as the one shown at top right is an invaluable aid in determining the tones of the scene you are painting, as it gives you a guide to assessing the tones of your subject by simply giving each area of colour a tonal value, depending on how light or dark it is. The scale illustrated here was produced using black ink, which I diluted to create the mid tones. This can then be added to a cardboard viewfinder, as shown on page 42, for quick reference when on location.

Another important consideration is the tonal key, which is the overall lightness or darkness of a painting and plays a vital role in establishing the overall atmosphere, emotion or mood of a picture. A predominantly light painting is said to have a high key, and a predominantly dark one a low key.

Painting *contre-jour* (against the light) can produce extremes of tone and make for dramatic paintings, as backlit objects are thrown into silhouette. Counterchange is another important factor, as the principles can be found throughout the landscape. Counterchange is simply the placing of light shapes against dark and vice versa, an effect that creates intriguing contrasts and makes for lively pictures.

When working in the studio from colour photographs, photocopy them in black and white. This helps to define the tonal value as well as simplifying the subject further. Once you learn to see colours in terms of tone, your paintings will greatly improve.

A black-and-white reproduction of the painting 'Rocks and Surf' shown below.

Rocks and Surf, Talland Bay
Watercolour and pastel
53 x 36cm (21 x 14in)
It is important to learn to see colours in terms of tone so that we can achieve unity in a painting by balancing the tonal 'weight' of one colour against that of another.

Talland Bay, Cornwall

Sensation

I always find painting the sea a challenging subject, and on this day its problems were particularly memorable. This was a seascape painting demonstration done for a group of students on a painting holiday in Cornwall.

We arrived on the beach on a hot and sunny afternoon in May; I looked around but could find little to inspire me, except the waves crashing on to some rocks and the stream running down the beach into the picture. Unfortunately, the tide was going out fast, so I knew that I would have little time to capture it.

What also made this view difficult was that the sun was behind me, making it a much more detailed and complicated subject than if I had been looking at it *contre-jour*.

These photographs show the scene chosen for the demonstration painting and my distance from it while painting.

Process

I used my viewfinder in order to decide on the format and to arrange the composition and focal point. I also found squinting at the scene helpful in defining the three-dimensional form and main shapes in the headland and rocks.

For this demonstration I used mixed media – watercolour and pastels combined on prestretched Bockingford watercolour paper. I drew in the composition using a black chisel-tip permanent pen and blocked in the main rocks, which would be my focal point. To reserve the highlights of the paper I used strips of torn masking tape, as shown on the right. If time had allowed I would have used masking fluid, but doing so would waste valuable time as it dried, as I could see the waves were diminishing each time that I looked up – these would finally have to be painted from memory, so I looked hard to try and retain as much information as I could. It is important to take the stickiness off the tape before applying it to the paper, otherwise it can rip the paper when you finally come to remove it – to counter this effect, I rub the tape between thumb and forefinger a few times.

Because I work with the board almost vertical, it was important to reserve the white areas from running paint. With a 2.5cm (1in) hake brush I applied strong washes of monestial blue, cadmium orange, raw sienna and burnt sienna, merging them together over the whole paper. The washes dried quickly in the sun and I applied further washes using the same colours. I also added black waterproof ink to the mixes for the beach and rocks. When this was dry I removed the masking tape.

Next came the pastels stage: I limited these to a small number and included light blue,

Stage 1
Torn pieces of masking tape are being applied to the initial drawing to reserve the highlights for the waves.

purple-greys, blue-violets, burnt sienna, sap green and dark brown. To cover larger areas I used the pastel on its side with broad strokes and blended some of these areas with my finger, particularly in the sky and stream. The firmer, more direct marks were left to suggest form and texture, especially in the rocks and beach.

Waves at Talland Bay
Watercolour and pastel
36 x 53cm (14 x 21in)

Swirling seagulls were flicked in with white and black conté crayons to add life and movement to the scene.

The tooth of the paper was useful here for the foreground as the broken colour gave a texture as well as contrast to the soft underlying washes of watercolour.

The eye is drawn to the focal point of the waves and rocks because of the strong contrasts of tone used in those areas of the painting.

Cliffs and Cove
Oils

Mullion Cove on the Lizard in Cornwall is an awe-inspiring place with a rugged coastline and a small, picturesque harbour. But what fascinates me about painting seascapes is the element of the unexpected – the change of light can affect the myriad of colours found in the sea and cliffs within seconds. This was the inspiration behind the small pen and watercolour sketch at right.

I decided on an almost square format for the painting, rather than a portrait view, as in the sketch, which meant that I had to think carefully about the composition, in particular the focal point. The high vantage point and horizon line helped to create a dramatic sense of depth and space to the scene.

Reference Sketch
Pen and watercolour • 18 x 13cm (7 x 5in)

materials

- MDF board prepared with gesso primer and paste

- Oils: cadmium orange, raw sienna, burnt sienna, ultramarine blue, cerulean blue, naples yellow, viridian, rose madder and titanium white

- Brushes: watercolour no. 4 round; 1.3cm (½in) and 0.6cm (¼in) soft flat wash

- Turpentine

- Rags

1 On a piece of hardboard primed with two coats of gesso primer and a third coat mixed with texture paste, I stained the board using a mix of cadmium orange and raw sienna and then rubbed it over with a rag to take some colour off. I sketched out the basic composition using a diluted mix of burnt sienna and ultramarine blue, applied with a soft No. 4 round brush.

2 Switching to a 1.3cm (½in) soft flat wash brush, I used the same mix to block in the cliff on the left, and then washed pure turps across this to help create texture as well as build up the tonal foundation. With a turps-laden rag I lifted off some of the background colour for the highlights in the sea (see above).

4 To establish colour in the sky (see below), I started with a mix of cerulean blue, rose madder and titanium white; as I brought this down from the top right of the picture, I added small amounts of Naples yellow and cerulean blue to the mix, and worked with a light touch – almost a drybrush effect – in order to allow some of the ground colour to show through.

3 I mixed viridian and rose madder for the cliffs, using a few strokes to make contours and indicate the darkest areas, and added marks for the dark rocks at the foot of the cliffs; I took care not to cover all the 'turpsy' effects. For the light marks on the smaller rocks I used the No. 4 round brush.

5 For the shadows in the sea at the base of the cliffs, particularly in the foreground, I applied a purple made from ultramarine blue and rose madder (see right and below).

6 With the 1.3cm (½in) wash brush I put in the mid greens, using a mix of viridian, raw sienna and a touch of rose madder; starting at the top of the cliffs, I worked down, brushing lightly and reducing the amount of paint on the brush, and added a bit more raw sienna to tone down the colour.

7 (See right) for the lights in the water, I started with a mix of ultramarine blue, titanium white and a touch of viridian, making broad, horizontal strokes towards the top of the sea; to get more definition I used the No. 4 round brush. After merging the sky and horizon together to leave no harsh demarcation line, I used a mix of viridian, titanium white and Naples yellow for the areas closer to the base of the cliffs.

Assessment

It was now time to stand back and take stock of where I was with the painting. I could see immediately that I needed to add more depth to it and in particular to address the foreground, middle ground and distance by using the principles of aerial perspective. Because of this, the colours and tonal value of the painting had to be adjusted. I decided to add warmer darks in the bottom left foreground and cooler colours, especially greens, in the distant headland. I was pleased with some of the textural effects in parts of the painting, but I realized that some of these might have to be painted over and sacrificed for the sake of the overall effect.

8 To establish some lights in the surf, I used a mix of titanium white and a very little Naples yellow, just indicating the highlights. Back with the larger flat brush, I stroked a warm purple, mixed from ultramarine blue, permanent rose and a touch of raw sienna, on the middle cliffs, using the edge of the brush to define the edge. To warm up the parts in shadow, I used a mix of ultramarine blue, cadmium orange, titanium white and a little rose madder.

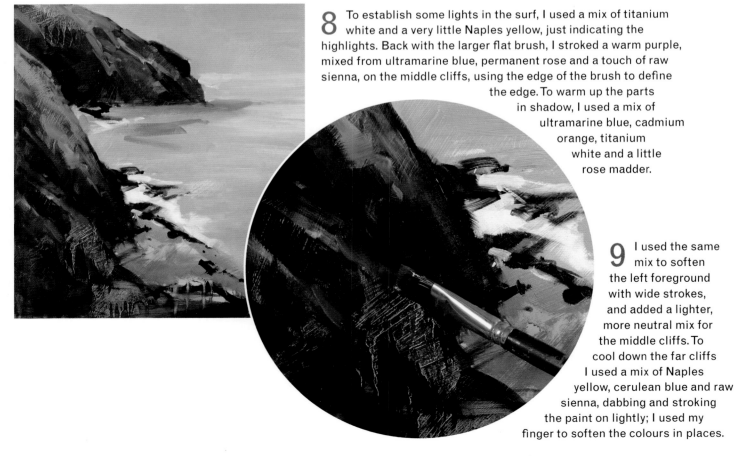

9 I used the same mix to soften the left foreground with wide strokes, and added a lighter, more neutral mix for the middle cliffs. To cool down the far cliffs I used a mix of Naples yellow, cerulean blue and raw sienna, dabbing and stroking the paint on lightly; I used my finger to soften the colours in places.

10 To bring shadow on to the beach area in the foreground, I used warm strokes of the warm mix from step 8, being careful to tone down the orange underlayer, not to lose it completely; I used my finger again to soften some of this colour.

11 For a suggestion of marks in the bottom left of the picture I used ultramarine blue and rose madder, blending it with a finger; then I did the same with a mix of cerulean blue and titanium white. For the shadow areas at the base of the cliffs I used a mix of ultramarine and rose madder. With a slightly darker version of the mix I painted negatively around the lightest parts, then used a mix of rose madder and titanium white for the tiny notches around the focal point and in the lower rocks, using a No. 4 round brush. I used titanium white with a touch of viridian in the centre of interest and along the shoreline (see left).

12 (See right) I used a mix of ultramarine blue and rose madder to block in more shadow areas at the bottom and in the middle cliffs, before putting more dark rocks in the foreground and dark areas on the furthest cliffs with a mix of ultramarine and burnt sienna. To give more form to the foreground I mixed ultramarine, rose madder and some titanium white.

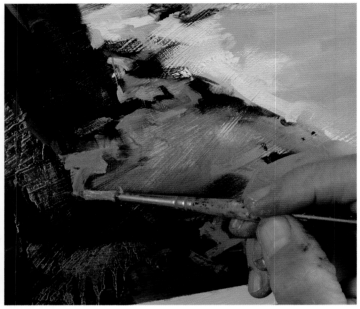

13 For a cool colour to knock back the prominent headland and introduce some aerial recession, I mixed ultramarine blue, rose madder and a touch of Naples yellow; while working across the far cliff with spare strokes, I made sure not to cover all the green. I then brought a mix of rose madder and titanium white down into the sea, again sparingly.

14 It was now time to add the finishing touches by putting in more lights: I lightly dragged a mix of titanium white and viridian across the sea, picking up the texture of the gesso ground. I used the same mix thickly, adding a little bit of ultramarine blue, to knock back the shoreline in the middle and make the strongest lights at the focal point in the top cove. To make waves breaking in the shadows below the furthest headland I used a mix of titanium white and a little ultramarine blue; painting negatively into the rocks, I brought this colour down into the main cove and further down the shoreline.

15 Some, but not all, of the underlayer near the shoreline needed to be covered: for the distant areas I used a light mix of viridian and titanium white, and nearer the foreground I mixed white and rose madder, each time blending the colours lightly with my finger.

Finished Painting
Cliffs and Cove
Oils
33 x 30cm (13 x 12in)
To help bring the foreground further forward I added detail to help suggest form and more defined edges in the cliff face by using the sharpened end of a brush handle. I also added a few seagulls set against the dark headland to help draw the eye further into the centre of interest, as well as to add life to the scene using the same technique. The sensual richness and physical nature of oils is the perfect medium for capturing the drama and beauty of these subjects.

Goose Rock, Crantock Bay
Watercolour and pastel
33 x 41cm (13 x 16in)
*This was a demonstration painting from the grounds
of the hotel I run painting courses at in Cornwall. I
was drawn to the mesmerizing colours in the sea and
foreground rockpools. Time is always a key factor, and the
urgency is evident in the brushstrokes – however, it also
gives energy to picture-making, which is so important.*

Mullion Cove, Cornwall
Watercolour and pastel
33 x 46cm (13 x 18in)
The spectacular situation of Mullion Cove on the Lizard, with its small harbour nestling beneath its towering cliffs, always makes for dramatic and interesting compositions.

Rocks at Cape Cornwall
Watercolour and pastel
48 x 48cm (19 x 19in)
*Like so many painters I find seascapes exhilarating, and
the subject touches all my senses. After all, where else
could one find more pleasurable sounds than that of
crashing waves and the cry of gulls?*

(Opposite below)
Sunlit Sea, Treyarnon
Watercolour and pastel
33 x 43cm (13 x 17in)
*I reserved the white paper for the highlights
with masking fluid. Most of the accent
colour was provided by pastels, while the
structural foundation of the painting was
put in with watercolour.*

**November
Afternoon at
Talland**
Watercolour and pastel
33 x 42cm (13 x 16in)
*This painting had
to be executed
quickly, partly
because of the
extreme weather
conditions – the
easel blew over
twice, despite
being weighted
down with my bag!*

CHAPTER EIGHT

Boats and Harbours

Newquay Harbour
Watercolour and pastel
33 x 41cm (13 x 16in)
I was attracted to the reflections left by the outgoing tide, and omitted a number of other boats that were in the scene.

'Painting must do for the eyes what poetry does for the ears.'

ANTOINE COYPEL

Painting amidst the sights and sounds of a bustling harbour has to be one of my favourite situations, the mere thought of which gets me reaching for my brushes! It's not only an ever-changing visual feast either: the sound of lapping water, the 'popping' mud on a falling tide, the calling gulls, the smell of seaweed, touch all the senses.

As mentioned earlier, the boats and harbours of the Exe estuary have provided me with much inspiration over the years, and my love affair with the subject has grown

further with numerous painting trips to Cornwall, where my favourite haunts are the harbours of Polperro and St Ives. Painters have long been inspired to paint in this remote part of Britain: influenced by the French Impressionists, painters arrived in the 1880s to paint *en plein air*, first in pursuit of realism. Artists' colonies were established at Newlyn and St Ives, and soon developed into the most significant art movements of recent times. It is a tradition that continues to thrive to this day.

The sketchbook

Harbours contain a wealth of complex material, and many students find the subject daunting for a number of reasons – for a start, many find drawing boats difficult.

You will need to put in a lot of sketchbook work in order to become familiar with the lines and shapes of the many different boats that you will find. Working in graphite pencil is ideal for doing this, as well as for quick studies to record fishermen, working on their boats or mending their nets, for instance.

To help simplify a scene and to organize the composition and tones, it's best to do a number of quick thumbnail sketches. I also like to sketch in a larger format by using fibre-tip pen and willow charcoal in an A3 cartridge pad. These quick sketches help you simplify and find the essentials in a subject, and prove invaluable if the tide comes in or goes out while you are still painting the scene. For location studies in colour, I use watercolour and gouache on a mid-tone tinted pastel paper.

First, however, I encourage students to spend an hour or so just drawing boats before they think about anything else. The first attempt is often shaky, but they soon get their eye in and confidence is quickly restored.

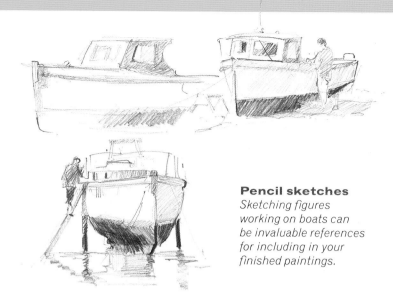

Pencil sketches
Sketching figures working on boats can be invaluable references for including in your finished paintings.

Polperro Harbour
(Above) Felt-tip pen and charcoal • 25 x 36cm (10 x 14in)
(Left) Watercolour and pastel • 53 x 36cm (21 x 14in)
Seeing the scene in terms of shapes and varying tones not only simplified the busy harbour scene, but also determined the compositional priorities more easily.

Choosing a medium

I enjoy working in most media for this subject, but my favourites have to be watercolour or mixed media (watercolour and pastels combined).Its fluidity and translucency make watercolour ideal, particularly for portraying the light, water, reflections and wet mud in particular. But it is also the perfect medium for painting the boats themselves – techniques such as wet-in-wet and drybrush are useful in suggesting not only the rust and texture on boats, but also the effects of reflected light, which can be so exciting.

When I use watercolour combined with pastels, the two media act as a catalyst, producing another dimension by adding a further variety of marks and textures, as well as depth, to the paintings.

Painting boats and harbours

Harbours at low tide interest me more than when the tide is fully in – tide pools and mud can add wonderful contrasts of colour, texture and shapes in the painting. As well as being interesting subjects themselves, seaweed, ropes and rusting chains can also help the composition, by directing your eye to the focal point. If it is high tide and you are painting boats in water, decide on the best position of the boat, be patient and work quickly.

I prefer painting boats at low tide for a number of reasons, most obviously because they don't move around and are not likely to be taken out on a fishing trip at any time. But the shapes of boats are more interesting at low tide too, particularly when you can see their hulls and keels. It is rare to find a 'ready-made' scene where boats are in the right place for you, so be prepared to move them around or leave them out of your picture altogether.

Don't be afraid to crop boats either: I often use a stern or bow of a boat to one side in order to frame, or lead the viewer's eye further into the picture. Showing a boat in this way creates a sense of space and intrigue and also hints at more beyond the confines of the picture. Introducing seagulls or a fisherman not only gives life and scale to the scene, but also a narrative content.

Making boats sit on the mud or float on the water is a common problem, as many students never make the shadows or reflections quite dark enough, so the boats tend to float in mid-

St Ives Harbour
Watercolour
18 x 20cm (7 x 8in)
You don't have to include every detail of rigging in a boat – here just a few lines suffice, and the viewer's eye suggests the rest.

Quayside, Watchet
Oils
36 x 25cm (14 x 10in)
The dark scene, emphasized by there being no sky visible, adds to the overall dramatic impact of this painting.

air instead. When working in watercolour I often merge a wet-in-wet wash of the keel into the sand or water, making it difficult to distinguish between the two. Another important factor is your viewpoint and eye level: you will find boats viewed from the quayside, looking down on them, more difficult, as you have to consider perspective and foreshortening.

When it comes to rigging, just indicate a few important areas, flicked in with a rigger brush or graphite pencil. Knowledge of boats and their rigging does help give authenticity, but too much detail will detract – it is far more important to capture the character of a boat.

Drawing Boats

Many students tend to draw what they know from experience, rather than what they see with their eyes; in desperation, some also look for shortcuts. However, observing both objectively and analytically is something you must learn to do, and this means measuring proportions and making constant comparisons. With practice this will soon become automatic, and before long you will see improvements.

For measuring, hold a pencil at arm's length, with the top of the pencil level with the top of the upright you are measuring. Then run your thumb down the pencil until it is level with the bottom of the subject. This will help you compare proportions as you draw; for example, the depth of the hull may fit four times into its length. The pencil can also be held horizontally.

If the boat is lying tilted on a low tide, look carefully at the angle of the mast or rudder to help you establish the correct tilt. Holding the pencil vertical at the scene, as well as drawing both vertical and horizontal pencil lines on the paper, can also be useful.

Seeing a boat enclosed in the shape of a box, as shown in the studies below, can be helpful in construction as well as perspective, and drawing a centre line from the bow to the stern can also be useful.

Drawing boats well does not rely on fully understanding their construction – however, it does help if you have a little knowledge of, or an interest in, the subject; and the more you do, the more you will know.

Measuring a boat using the pencil and thumb technique

In a side view of a boat at eye level, the gunwale on the far side appears much straighter, even though you know it is curved.

Hold a pencil or viewfinder horizontally at arm's length against the top of the transom to help check the correct tilt of the boat.

Observe the curved lines of the boat carefully – don't make them rise too steeply.

Horizon/eye level

Horizon/eye level

Think of a boat enclosed in the shape of a box. This also helps with perspective and especially with foreshortening.

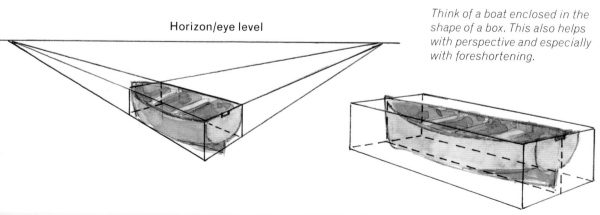

OCTOBER 2001

Polperro Harbour, Cornwall

Sensation

Polperro Harbour has always been one of my favourite locations to visit. On a sunny day in October, with a typically complex view of fishing boats in the outer harbour, my initial interest in the scene was the colours and textures to be found in the mud, which contrasted with the tide pools reflecting the harbour wall. I also found the shadows and colours in the reflected light on the white fishing boat particularly exciting.

My first priority on arrival at any harbour is to find out the state of the tide, for obvious reasons. I learned from a fisherman that I had about an hour before the tide would be back in again, so decided that a quick location study in watercolour and gouache would be appropriate for a painting.

Process

I used my viewfinder to help decide on the format and composition, and settled on a landscape format, with the red fishing boat my main focal point and the other boats simply framing the scene.

I positioned the main boat in the upper Golden Section of the picture in order to concentrate on the interest in the foreground, and raised the horizon line so as not to include the buildings on the quayside.

For this study I used prestretched moonstone Canson Mi-Teintes pastel paper; I sketched out the initial drawing with a graphite pencil, and then reserved some shapes in the foreground mud with masking fluid.

When the fluid was dry I applied light washes of Naples yellow, cerulean blue, permanent rose and raw sienna watercolour to the buildings and harbour wall, allowing the soft pink colour of the paper to show through in places.

I then added permanent white gouache to state the highlights on the boats, and a mix of ultramarine and burnt umber for the darks on the boat on the left. This helped me evaluate the tonal values between the two easily.

I now added a mix of cerulean and permanent rose to the shadowed area of the boats, keeping this as transparent as possible to allow the underlying warmth of the paper colour to show through. When I next looked up, the tide was on its way in at speed and I knew that the whole scene would be completely different very soon – if you wish to speed up your painting skills, then painting in a harbour is certainly one sure way of practising!

I used cadmium red on the boat, adding a touch of white gouache to lighten the highlights, and a mix of cerulean and raw sienna for the gunwale and keel for the other boat. I brought these colours down into the foreground, and when this was dry, I rubbed off the masking fluid.

Now the boats were floating there was no mud, so I decided to add some reflections. However, usually in circumstances such as this, above everything else it is important to try and remain faithful to the original idea.

These photographs show the view of the harbour chosen for the final location study.

106

Fishing Boats, Polperro
Felt-tip pen and charcoal
25 x 36cm (10 x 14in)
*I produced this quick charcoal
sketch while I was waiting for the
initial wash of watercolour to dry
in the damp conditions. Delays are
always frustrating, but it provided
me with a useful reference,
particularly when the tide came
in much sooner than expected.*

Fishing Boats, Polperro
Watercolour and gouache
25 x 36cm (10 x 14in)
This is the finished location study.

Incoming Tide
Watercolour and gouache

Busy harbours, such as St Ives in Cornwall, are always inspirational and exciting places to paint, but because of their complexities they can often be daunting subjects. In this studio demonstration painting, I used as reference a simple monochrome sketch done in charcoal and felt-tip pen. I felt that the composition worked well and if I could create in paint what had inspired me – namely the unique light and reflections on an ebbing tide – then it would be plain sailing! But watercolour being the unpredictable medium that it is, I knew that the painting would need much forward planning if it were to succeed. Despite this, I knew that choosing watercolour was the perfect medium for capturing those transient effects of light in sky and water.

materials

- 4B graphite pencil
- 300gsm (140lb) Not Whatman prestretched paper
- Watercolours: cadmium orange, Naples yellow, winsor blue, cerulean blue, permanent rose, raw sienna, cadmium red, burnt umber, sap green
- Gouache: permanent white
- Brushes: old brush for masking fluid; 2.5cm (1in) hake; Nos 6 and 10 round; No.1 rigger
- Masking fluid
- Masking tape
- Plastic ruler

Reference sketch
Felt-tip pen and charcoal
28 x 36cm (11 x 14in)
The composition, tonal values and balance worked well in the sketch, so there was little need to change anything. I left out a number of boats from the original view and decided that my main focus of interest was the boat on the left; I therefore constructed the rest of the painting around it. The overall scene, including the background, was suitably simplified in the sketch, to help when it came to creating the painting in colour.

1 After putting in the pencil drawing outline with a 4B graphite pencil, I stuck masking tape around the picture and then applied masking fluid with an old brush to reserve the highlights.

2 I began by laying in broad washes of a thin mix of cadmium orange and Naples yellow, applying bold, sweeping strokes over the whole of the paper with a 2.5cm (1in) hake brush.

3 For the sky and the water I merged Winsor blue into the first mix on the paper to set the overall mood for the painting, dropping a little raw sienna into the sand in the foreground.

4 When these washes were dry I applied a thin transparent mix of raw sienna and Winsor blue to the distant hills, keeping this colour on the cool side; this helped to minimize the impact and gave the impression of recession. While this was wet I added a mix of Winsor blue and cadmium red at the base of the hills. The reflections were applied with a medium round brush (No. 10) using vertical strokes, with wet-in-wet mixes of the same colours diluted with plenty of water, so as not to make the reflections too opaque. After putting a light wash of cerulean blue and permanent rose on the boat hulls, I let everything dry thoroughly.

5 I applied a further mix of cerulean blue and permanent rose in the middle distance to suggest recession for the hills in the far distance.

6 After putting in a splash of cadmium red on the boat on the left, I strengthened the hull of the right-hand boat with a wash of cadmium red and Winsor blue, and used stronger mixes of the same colours for the shadows of both boats, to sit them more firmly into the wet sand. I then removed the masking tape around the edges of the picture and stood back for a preliminary assessment before replacing the tape.

7 Using my finger I gently rubbed off the masking fluid to reveal the white paper. You can see how effective these highlights are, and the 'sparkle' of the reserved paper is immediately evident. I left a small amount of masking fluid untouched around the left hand boat in order to lay a further wash for the reflections over this.

8 With much of the masking fluid removed, I felt that there were now too many glaringly white highlights, so I toned down some of these with a mix of cerulean blue and permanent rose, so that they became an integral part of the scene. This wash was also added below the boat on the right to suggest the shadow and reflections.

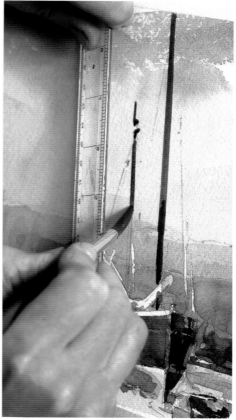

9 The masts were put in with the No.10 round brush with a dark mix of burnt umber and Winsor blue; in order to get them straight, I used a ruler on its side and ran the ferrule of the brush along it. Switching to a fine (No. 1) rigger brush and using the ruler again, I painted in the rigging with the same colour, working almost drybrush.

TIP
To keep masts and rigging straight hold a plastic ruler at a slight angle and guide the ferrule of the brush along its edge.

Assessment

I removed the masking tape around the edge of the painting to help me evaluate the overall picture. The basic structure was sound, but tonally it still lacked contrast. I looked hard at my sketch and also squinted at both painting and sketch to see what further work was needed – in particular the foreground sand needed to be strengthened for the background to recede further. The reflections needed to be put in much more strongly, particularly around the left hand boat, which I had decided to have as my centre of interest.

10 I applied a warm wash of cerulean blue, permanent rose and raw sienna to the sand. When this was dry I added texture using the drybrush technique with raw sienna straight from the tube; this allowed the paint to catch the tooth of the paper and create an interesting texture to the sand. While this was wet, I used a wash of sap green for the rope in the right foreground. To darken the water I made a light and then a medium wash of cerulean blue, and then added a mix of cerulean and rose wash for the reflections of the boats.

11 Using mainly downward strokes with my hake brush, I applied a strong wash of burnt umber with a touch of winsor blue for the reflections of the distant hills and right hand boat. When this was dry I removed the remaining masking fluid with my finger.

12 It is always a problem knowing when to stop, particularly if you have enjoyed the process of painting: the best tip at this stage is to leave it for a few minutes and come back to it with a fresh eye. I added the ropes and some more rigging to the boats using a graphite pencil and a rigger brush, and further details were included using white gouache – in some cases with watercolour added to the white. I spattered some paint into the foreground sand to add further texture, and finally flicked in some seagulls with a graphite pencil and a rigger brush loaded with white gouache. This not only added an element of life to the painting, but also helped draw the eye to the focal point.

Finished painting
Incoming Tide
Watercolour and gouache
29 x 38cm (11½ x 15in)

This painting brings together a number of traditional watercolour techniques, including layered washes, wet-into-wet and drybrush; masking fluid was used to preserve the highlights. Keeping the colours spontaneous, fresh and transparent, in addition to taking risks, is the essence of the medium. The translucency of the paint takes full advantage of a scene such as this, creating a feeling of light and air.

Porthleven Harbour
Watercolour
13 x 18in (5 x 7in)

This small watercolour captures the essence of the early morning light in a Cornish harbour. The highlights of the paper, wet-in-wet washes and texture created by the drybrush technique give an atmosphere of which only this medium is capable.

Lerryn
Watercolour and pastel
33 x 41cm (13 x 16in)
Lerryn, in Cornwall, is a favourite spot for painters from all over Britain, and it is not difficult to see why. This painting shows to good effect the combination of watercolour and pastels working together to convey a real atmosphere to this peaceful scene.

Still Day, Kildonan, Isle of Arran
Watercolour and pastel
35 x 38cm (14 x 15in)
To echo the tranquillity and ethereal light in this scene I wanted the watercolour underpainting to prevail. I used a limited palette of watercolours and then added pastels to create further contrast and texture.

Water's Edge
Watercolour and pastel
43 x 43cm (17 x 17in)
The inspirations behind this more intimate harbour painting were the colours to be found in the shadows, the wet mud and the reflections. I chose a square format for this painting, as I felt doing so would make for a more interesting composition.

Porthleven Harbour
Oils
25 x 36cm (10 x 14in)
Although this painting was done on location, I decided to simplify the busy background in the studio. I try not to do this too often, as I invariably overwork the picture. 'Letting go' when you are enjoying the process is not easy, but it is essential if you are not to lose the spontaneity of the original work.

Conclusion

Sunlit Creek, Lerryn
Watercolour and pastel
43 x 46cm (17 x 18in)
This was a most inspiring subject as the bright sunlight bathed the deep wooded creek. The dramatic light was further enhanced by the deep, foreground shadows in the water and mudbanks.

As with all journeys, this one must come to an end. I hope that you have enjoyed reading this book as much as I have producing it. You will find the road that lies ahead for you is full of new discoveries and fresh challenges, whether in exploring a new medium, a new technique – or even a completely new subject.

In the landscape you may be drawn more to the natural remoteness of a scene or perhaps intrigued more by man's influence on his environment in the towns and cities. The technique may mean you prefer to work in the studio from sketches, rather than paint on location. After all, painting comes in many different guises and is open to individual interpretation, whether this is towards realism or abstraction.

It doesn't really matter which route you take, as your choices will reflect ultimately what appeals to you personally. My paintings and views are constantly changing, evolving and finding new directions, and this is how it should be, of course. Through the subject of landscape and exploring the different media available, I find a diversity that keeps my work 'alive' as well as my life interesting.

One of the most important qualities in painting is the personal statement of a painter; it is this that distinguishes his or her work from others. As we have seen, this means looking around you, as well as inside yourself, in order to find what interests and moves you. I hope that through these pages I have come some way to showing you what moves me, and perhaps have planted a few ideas in fertile soil along the way. Of course, as with any creative pursuit there will be highs and lows and even times when you feel you are going backwards – we've all been there, whatever level you are at! Travelling along your own path can be a lonely experience, so working with fellow artists, as well as getting feedback from them, is an important ingredient in the painting process.

The sensitivity between the artist and the landscape is the vital ingredient to painting landscapes with atmosphere. As you embark on your journey, think on the words the great American artist and teacher Robert Henri once said: 'Everything depends on the attitude of the artist towards his subject. It is the one great essential. It is on this attitude of the artist towards his subject that the real quality of the picture, its significance, and the nature and distinction of its technique depends. If your attitude is negligent, if you are not awake to the possibilities you will not see them. Nature does not reveal herself to the negligent.'

Whatever your eventual goal and path that you take, be sure to enjoy the journey itself. The directions and possibilities are limitless. However, if you should get lost or perhaps take a short cut that results in a dead end, just follow your own instincts and listen to your inner voice. This will lead you then to follow the signpost that says: 'Your way'!

Scottish Glen
Watercolour and pastel
48 x 36cm (19 x 14in)
Working on location encourages you to 'think on your feet,' enabling you to work more economically and to simplify complicated subjects.

Further Reading

Other books by Ray Balkwill

Watercolour Plus, David & Charles 2002

Ray Balkwill's Exe Estuary, Halsgrove 2004

Learn to Paint: Coastal Landscapes, HarperCollins, 2006

Art and instruction books featuring Ray Balkwill's work

Bulgin, Sally, *The Artist's Practical Problem Solver*, HarperCollins 2003

Bulgin, Sally, *Artists' Rescue Tactics*, HarperCollins 2005

Hosegood, Betsy, *Paint! Seascapes and Waterways*, RotoVision 2001

Jelbert, Wendy and Sidaway, Ian, *The Encyclopedia of Watercolour*, Lorenz Books 2003

Jennings, Simon, *Art Class*, HarperCollins 1999

Jennings, Simon, *Artist's Colour Manual*, HarperCollins 2003

Le Messurier, Brian, *Dartmoor Artists*, Halsgrove 2002

Articles by Ray Balkwill

The Artist magazine

1995: December – 'Painting Estuaries and Harbours in Watercolour'
1997: May – 'Adventures in Mixed Media'
      July – 'Sketching Boats and Harbours'
      August – 'On the Waterline: Boats and Harbours in Watercolour'
1998: April – 'Painting Skies in Pastel'
      October – 'First Impressions in Oils'
1999: January – 'Irish Skies and Italian Colour'
2000: July/August – 'Painting Seascapes in Mixed Media'
2001: April – 'Changing Light in the Landscape'
2002: June – 'Tide Lines: Boats and Harbours'
2003: March – 'Painting Skies'
      September – 'Out in the Wilderness'
2004: October – 'A Sense of Place: The Exe Estuary'
      December – 'Rescue Tactics: In Reflective Mood'
2006: March – 'Mountains and Sea'

International Artist magazine

1998: June – 'Painting Seascapes in Mixed Media'
1999: June – 'Masters of the Media' by Ron Ranson

Pastel Artist International magazine

2000: May – 'United Kingdom Showcase'

An art instruction film featuring Ray Balkwill painting on the Exe estuary, *Capturing Estuary Moods*, is available from APV Films, tel: 01608 641798.
For further details about Ray Balkwill visit: www.raybalkwill.co.uk

Acknowledgments

The preparation and production of this book have involved many people, and I am grateful to them all for their cooperation. In particular I would like to thank my commissioning editor, Freya Dangerfield, for her faith, enthusiasm and invaluable help in its production. Thanks, too, go to Sarah Underhill, Lisa Wyman and Louise Clark at David & Charles for the design and editing, to Ian Kearey for his editorial skills, and to Nigel Cheffers-Heard for his fine photography. It has been a great pleasure for me to work with the publishers of this book.

I am also grateful to Sally Bulgin, editor of *The Artist* magazine, for allowing me to use extracts from past articles of mine for the Diary Showcases. Thanks go to the following, who have kindly supplied photographs of me painting on location: Tom Burley, Ann Fellows, Dr Judy Harrington, David Rouse, James Treglown and Pauline Weller.

I greatly appreciate the interest from the many students who return each year from all over the country to join me on my painting courses; they in turn have inspired me to put my artistic journey into words in the form of this book.

And finally, my sincere thanks to my patrons who allowed the reproduction of paintings from their private collections and have continued to support me over the years.

Index